D0541148

SPORTING LIVES

SPORTING LIVES

—

MICHAEL
PARKINSON

PAVILION

All these articles originally appeared in the *Daily Telegraph*

My thanks to Sports Editor of the *Daily Telegraph*, David Welsh, and to
Nigel Seymour for their help, encouragement and unfailing good humour.

MP

First published in Great Britain in 1993 by
PAVILION BOOKS LIMITED
26, Upper Ground, London SE1 9PD

Text copyright © Michael Parkinson 1992

Illustrations by Andrew Farmer
Designed by Nigel Partridge

The moral right of the author has been asserted

All rights reserved. No part of this publication may be reproduced, stored in a
retrieval system, or transmitted, in any form or by any means, electronic,
mechanical, photocopying, recording or otherwise, without the prior permission of
the copyright holder.

A CIP catalogue record for this book is available from the British Library.

ISBN 1 85793 089 4

Printed and bound in England by Butler & Tanner Ltd

2 4 6 8 10 9 7 5 3

This book may be ordered by post direct from the publisher.
Please contact the Marketing Department.
But try your bookshop first.

CONTENTS

PREFACE

'Personally, I have always looked upon cricket as organized loafing'
WILLIAM TEMPLE, Archbishop of Canterbury, 1925

'Boxing is showbusiness with blood'
DAVID BELASCO, American impresario, 1915

*'To think of football as merely twenty-two hirelings kicking a ball is merely to say
that a violin is wood and cat gut, Hamlet is so much ink and paper. It is
Conflict and Art'*
J. B. PRIESTLEY

*'One of the beautiful things about sports is going all out, playing with total
abandonment, your entire being, your mind and body integrated. But when it's over,
it's over. It was a game, not World War III'*
JACK SCOTT, American sports administrator

*'I think that to be clocking into a factory would be the worst thing in the world. All
you would say to the man next to you is, "What's in your sandwich, Charlie?"'*
RODNEY MARSH, footballer, 1967

'The ball is man's most disastrous invention, not excluding the wheel'
ROBERT MORLEY, actor, 1965

*'I am here to propose a toast to the sportswriters. It's up to you whether you
stand or not'*
FRED TRUEMAN

'We work in the toy department'
JIMMY CANNON, American sportswriter, explaining his craft

'I have nothing to add, except read on'
MICHAEL PARKINSON, 1992

For a couple of weeks now the birds have been flying southwest over our cricket ground, heading, no doubt, for the World Cup. The leaves are drifting across the square and the wind is not as gentle as it was.

There is an edge to it and you feel it on your face like astringent. Time to go. Time to hand over to hockey. There have been other signs too. Last week, after an exhilarating run chase, our last man went to the wicket with the team needing six to win.

The captain had told him to go for the runs. He blocked the first ball as if defending for his life. He stretched forward to the next one which he missed and the stumper removed the bails. "Not out," said the umpire, whereupon the skipper, understandably miffed at his orders being ignored, shouted: "Have a go".

At this point the batsman walked towards the pavilion brandishing his bat and saying words to the effect that if the skipper could do any better he should take his place in the middle.

He had advanced only three paces from his crease and was in the middle of his peroration when the keeper, who really did think he had stumped him and was still in possession of a bail, pulled out a stump and appealed again to the umpire who gave the batsman run out. I will be discreet about what ensued, except to say that it ended in laughter rather than tears, with jugs being bought by batsman and keeper alike. It was, however, the clearest sign so far that the gods were growing weary and we must be on our way.

Where to go? What to do until next April? These questions were easier to answer when I was young. When I was at school the change of seasons meant switching ambitions from opening for England with Len Hutton to nodding in crosses supplied by Tom Finney. When I first started work as a journalist it meant transferring my hero worship from Neville Cardus to 'Old International'.

I wonder how many remember the contribution made to the Manchester Guardian (as it was then) and BBC Sports Report by Don

Davies, or "Old International", as the Guardian insisted on disguising him.

When we discuss the great sports writers and commentators he rarely gets a mention and yet, in my view, his contribution to soccer was as important and as distinctive as Arlott's to cricket.

It is a hard claim to justify except by memory because very little of his work is available in collected form. Perhaps it is time some enterprising publisher invaded the archives to remind us of a unique journalist.

More than most observers, but in common with the best, he saw soccer as a vivid interplay between players and spectators. With a shrewd eye on the field of play, he also kept an ear cocked for the illuminating quote. It was he who told us of the man on the terraces at his beloved Bolton who, after watching one player spending all afternoon trying to beat opponents and failing, said to his neighbour: "But why doesn't he learn how to dribble. He's got nothing else to do."

In the days of goalposts made of iron he reported a penalty kick striking the bar with such ferocity that the frame hummed like a tuning fork for some time after. He began one report in the Guardian: "Happy is said to be the family which can eat onions together. They are for the time being separate from the world and have a harmony of aspiration. So it was with the scoring of goals at Old Trafford on Saturday." He loved the great creative players. Of Wilf Mannion he wrote: "Mannion is Mozartian in his exquisite workmanship. His style is so graceful and so courtly that he wouldn't be out of place if he played in a lace ruffle and the peruque."

Reporting from Maine Road about a bad day for Manchester City, he told his BBC audience: "City's defence line are a fine statuesque lot, but what's the good of that, Albert Square is full of 'em." He collected eccentrics, particularly goalkeepers. It was Davies who first pointed out that it wasn't necessary for goalkeepers to have a slate loose, but it helped.

He told of Iremonger, a tall and lanky goalkeeper for Notts County, who once persuaded his skipper to let him take a penalty kick. Iremonger ran the length of the field and hit the bar with such force that the ball rebounded back over his head. Iremonger set off back towards his own goal pursued by a pack of forwards and in his eagerness to kick the ball clear scored a spectacular own goal from 30 yards.

Davies was aided and abetted in his job by the nature of the game at that time. He perished in the Manchester United air disaster but his career embraced Billy Meredith and Bryan Douglas, Dixie Dean and John Charles, Alex James and Len Shackleton. It was a time of great individual artistry, when players were given the licence to be whimsical, even eccentric.

I never met Donny Davies and yet I felt I knew him very well indeed. We overlapped for a while when I joined the Manchester Guardian, but I never saw him in the office. I did see Cardus. I was on duty late one night making telephone calls around the local police and fire brigades when he made an entrance and sat composing at the typewriter. I watched quietly from afar as he ripped page after page from the machine and threw it in the waste paper basket. I knew that when he had finished and departed that the key to the secret of writing lay in the basket.

When he left the room I collected the contents of the waste paper basket and took them to my corner of the room where I unfurled them to read the words he had rejected. On every sheet – and there must have been 20 – was written 'Cardus. Page 1' and nothing else. So much for the secrets of inspiration. I never spoke to Cardus. Like Davies, I worshipped from afar. They will never know how much I admired them and how much they fuelled my young ambition.

My problem was that I couldn't make up my mind to do either one thing or the other, which is to say play the sport or write about it. For a time I tried both. As a 16-year-old reporter on a local paper and centre forward for a local team I was in the unique position to write about my own performance. I didn't exactly sell myself short. Very soon headlines like "Parkinson On The Goal Trail Again" became commonplace.

Even when I didn't figure on the scoresheet I made sure the report reflected the part I played in the game thus: "Ace goalscorer Mike Parkinson took an afternoon off from hitting the back of the net last week but was the brains behind his team's 6–0 win. . . ." Any stranger I saw on the touchline automatically became a scout from a League club in the following week's paper. "Three scouts, believed to be from Barnsley, Wolverhampton Wanderers and Manchester United, were at the game keeping a close eye on goalscoring hot-shot Mike Parkinson. . . ."

Eventually, intrigued by reports of them being where they had never thought of going, the real scouts started turning up. At one game there were representatives from every League club in the north of England to see this young centre forward, who, if you believed what the local paper said about him, was at least as good as Nat Lofthouse.

They left at half-time and never came back, but even this had little effect upon fantasy. I wrote that "Offers are expected within the next few days for free-scoring Mike Parkinson from representatives of several League clubs who were greatly impressed by the young centre forward. . . ." I would have continued undeterred had it not been for the fact that in addition to reporting the doings of my own team I had, alas, to collect results from the entire area to phone through to the Sunday papers.

This involved me leaping on to my cycle at the end of a game and hurtling around the local clubs. I had about an hour from the end of the game to cycle 12 miles around the local teams and phone the results through. I might not have been able to play like Nat Lofthouse but I soon had legs like him.

The problem of transferring the fantasy from professional soccer players to ace journalist was mainly one of wardrobe. I have always been one for a uniform and what was needed to transform me was a change of costume. I was much influenced in my idea of what journalists wore by watching Humphrey Bogart movies in which he always dressed in snap-brim trilby and belted raincoat. I bought both. The raincoat wasn't a problem but the trilby was. There weren't too many snap-brimmed, pearl-grey trilbys to be found at gents outfitters in Barnsley in those days.

When eventually I found one the larger problem became the question of how I kept it on my head. It was all very well for Mr Bogart but he never had to cycle around South Yorkshire in a force nine gale in his trilby hat.

Eventually I patented a chin strap from a length of knicker elastic and became not simply the only person in all the South Yorkshire coalfield to own a pearl-grey, snap-brimmed trilby, but the only person on the planet who attached it to his head with a chinstrap made from material which normally held up ladies' drawers.

Ludicrous though I must have looked, I was too cocooned in fantasy to know nor care what others thought. I was quite literally brought down to earth pedalling downhill into a stiff wind in search of results when the trilby flew from my head and acted like an arresting

parachute on a returning space shuttle.

You could argue that the incident became a metaphor for my entire life. What I do know is that it was a perfect demonstration of the difference between man's aspiration and his achievements and that the trick of keeping sane is never to forget how risible we really are.

If Don Davies had one gift it was that he kept reminding us of this fact. The wonderful aspect of having heroes is not that we ever match their achievements – that is not the point. The important part is that so long as we have them we spend time in the best possible company.

When I first started writing about the Barnsley footballers of my youth, it was in the mid-1960s and football still had a few discernible links with the past. To be reminded of them today is not so much to conjure up ghostly figures in a distant landscape as to try to describe creatures from another planet.

I am writing this on the day someone circulated details that Mr Gascoigne will make 10 million quid from the game. At the same time, the new superstar of British soccer was celebrating the news by reportedly telling an interviewer that George Best was a drunken bum and a disgrace to the game. Mr Gascoigne should remember there are those of us who are able to make comparisons and whose best advice would be to tell Gazza to keep his mouth zipped and concentrate on totting up the money while counting his blessings.

Way before George arrived on the scene, there were players in British football who could certainly teach Gazza a thing or two about playing soccer. What is more, some of them played for Barnsley. They are described in a book called *Oakwell Centurions* by David Watson.

The book is of little significance unless you happened to spend your formative years, as I did, on the terraces of Oakwell. Then it becomes a testament to our lost youth and a reaffirmation that although nostalgia might colour a memory it rarely distorts it.

For instance, I have been accused of inventing a soccer player called Skinner Normanton. Mr Watson not only removes this foul slur from my reputation but further made my day by revealing that Sid (to give him his Sunday name) is still alive and well and growing sunflowers as tall as goalposts at his home near Barnsley.

This news will be greeted with incredulity by those who played against him and lived to tell the tale. The thought that Skinner might have a gentle, caring side to his nature was not apparent to the players who received his close attention, not to mention his fans at Barnsley who used to warn their children: "If you don't behave we'll send for Skinner."

He was not a skilful player but he was good at stopping people who thought they were. His added dimension was his identification with the home crowd. He was carved from the coal they dug. He was as plain and functional as a cloth cap.

He had, however, a certain style based on his lack of pretensions. Towards the end of his career, after he had been injured by another hard man called Alex Forbes in a cup tie at Highbury, he played his comeback games in the old Midland League.

It was not a league for fainthearts. Barnsley were playing a colliery side comprised of players who shared Skinner's simple philosophy that football was a man's game.

They started the game vigorously and had kicked several Barnsley players over the wall when Skinner decided to exert his authority. He stood with foot on ball and beckoned a challenge. Three of the opposition accepted. When the dust settled Skinner was seen still with foot on ball while the three defenders were stretched out on the turf. The referee ran over, pulling out his notebook, whereupon Skinner held up a hand in a placatory gesture and said: "Tha' needn't bother ref, I'm going." And then he left the field.

They weren't all like that, my heroes, who played for Barnsley. There were the skilful ones like Cec McCormack, who came and went as mysteriously as Shane; Danny Blanchflower, who came to Oakwell from Glentoran before moving on to Aston Villa, Tottenham Hotspur and his own place in the pantheon. He told me once that when he first came to Barnsley he played a practice game with Skinner in the opposition. Skinner won the ball and moved upfield and Danny positioned himself to intercept. As he did so he reminded himself that this was the Second Division of the Football League and the players were likely to be possessed of a larger repertoire of tricks than he had been used to at Glentoran.

He was pondering the alternatives when he found himself flat on his back with stud marks up his front where Skinner had simply walked over him. It was a fair introduction. Later on, when Danny had left the club, Skinner achieved the unique distinction of being sent off by the manager during a practice game for roughing up one of his team-mates.

Dear Skinner – he'd put the wind up Gazza. May his sunflowers flourish.

Mr Watson's book, or that part of it dealing with the immediate post-war years and the 1950s, is not simply a catalogue of players and what has become of them. It's a reminder of a time when it was pleasant to go to a football match, when the crowd would be exhilarated by victory and crestfallen by defeat, but would not be persuaded by either emotion to have a punch-up.

It was a time when the players earned as much, or as little, as the people who watched them and if you got an early bus to the game you might sit next to one of your heroes. I have never recovered from the fact that I once sat next to Johnny Kelly on a bus. As a major event in my life, this was only surpassed by the occasion, much later, when I shared a seat on public transport with Tom Finney.

When I tell you that, Matthews and Finney apart, Kelly was the finest winger I have seen, you will think I am mad – but then you probably didn't see him play. It has always been my belief, which Mr Watson supports, that Kelly changed the face of English soccer.

He did so by making a monkey out of Alf Ramsey when Sir h'Alf, as he later became, was a full-back for Southampton. It was October 2, 1948, on a wet and miserable day, when Kelly established such a dominance over his opponent that had it been a boxing match it would have been called off at half-time.

It was my theory that later, Sir Alf sought his revenge on wingers to the point when he became a manager, he got rid of them. It would be nice if it were true because it would give Kelly his proper place in the history of the game.

As it is, his claim to fame is that he was possibly the only footballer to have a bleach named after him. While at Barnsley, he manufactured Kelzone, advertised in the local programme as: "The 100 per cent bleach cleanser and purifier – a boon to the housewife and honest value for money."

The product was manufactured in the back yard of a pub and the man who put his name to it also humped it on to the back of a lorry and sold it.

It is no secret that Mr Kelly did this without the assistance of an agent, a lawyer, a tax expert, a public relations man and two bodyguards. Nor did he sell himself or his product by cuddling Prime Ministers or being seen in the presence of bimbos. In those simple days of my youth we bought Kelzone because we knew that if it was half as good as the man who made it we would have the cleanest kit in the country. In those days a boy could trust his heroes.

The debate in soccer about moving the goalposts is nothing new. It was already a fully-fledged issue when I started playing back street soccer nearly 50 years ago.

In those days the rules stated that the goal should be as wide as the size of the goalkeeper times three. This required the goalie to lie down while we placed a coat at his feet and repeat the process twice more whereupon we put the other coat at his head. This meant there were not many tall goalkeepers to be found in our league. They all tended to be on the dwarfish side of small.

Size was also important in judging where the crossbar was. In those days crossbars were only owned by proper football clubs so we had to make an agreed assessment of where it might be in relation to the goalkeeper's height.

The arguments over whether a shot would have hit the crossbar, cleared it or even hit the underside and bounced down over the line sometimes verged on the metaphysical but invariably ended in violence and tears. We solved the problem by learning to keep the ball low when shooting.

My father told me that he once saw Steve Bloomer, a prolific goalscorer for Middlesbrough, take a penalty against "Tiny" Foulkes, the Sheffield United goalkeeper, who was a huge man weighing about 20 stone, on a wet and soggy day at Bramall Lane when the ball was like a lead shot.

Bloomer, who was renowned for his strength, struck the ball straight at Foulkes's midriff whereupon, having caught the ball, the goalkeeper was propelled over the goalline into the back of the net like a man skiing backwards. My old man reckoned Steve Bloomer was doing it for a bet. But I knew that it was the supreme example of a tactic learned during an apprenticeship in backyard soccer.

The only time we had a proper framework for a goal was when we dared to play against the garage door at the top of our street. Not unnaturally, the man who owned it objected to his freshly painted door being used as a target by muddy footballs so games had a tendency to be interrupted. But the joy of seeing the imprint of your match-winning shot on the green woodwork remains with me to this day.

Indeed when I rose to head Sippy Salt's cross into the top right hand corner to beat Gonk Reynolds's team by the odd goal of 33, it was the proudest moment of my life. It didn't matter that my run towards the Royal Box was interrupted by the garage owner who prevented me receiving the Cup from my King by chasing me across two fields and threatening to send for PC Williams. PC Williams was feared by every youngster who visited Barnsley FC in those days. And a lot of us did.

Just after the war, 20,000 spectators at Oakwell was an average gate. PC Williams would stroll around the field before the game to demonstrate his presence. On the odd occasion there was a disturbance in the crowd he would approach the incident and beckon with his forefinger at the offender who would voluntarily give himself up and be escorted around the ground and out of it by the constable.

The only time the matter might be taken further was if the culprit failed to obey the beckoning finger. This would necessitate PC Williams making – for him – two extravagant and unnecessary gestures, namely laying his cape on the turf and then hopping over the wall into the crowd. When this happened you could be sure that the offender was not seen for a month or two at home matches, having been warned off by the good constable. FIFA should find PC Williams and seek his views on security at the next World Cup.

Thinking of Sippy Salt reminded me of another important contribution that backyard soccer leagues made to more entertaining soccer . . . the closet winger. These were the wingmen who employed their skills by flicking the ball against the closet wall, racing past the opponent, and taking the return pass off the brickwork. Stanley Matthews was a closet winger, so was Tom Finney. Johnny Kelly, at Barnsley, was another.

By the way, having written about Kelly recently – particularly about the way he shaped the future of English soccer by giving Alf Ramsey a terrible time when Southampton came to Barnsley, thereby creating Sir h'Alf's hatred of wingers – a historian of the game asked if I could give a date for this momentous event. It was October 2, 1948, and the Barnsley team was Pat Kelly, Williams, Pallister; Normanton, Whyte, Glover; Smith, Griffiths, Robledo, Baxter and Johnny Kelly.

I also recall Southampton had a goalkeeper called Black, that Ramsey was right fullback, that Ted Bates played inside-forward, Charlie Wayman was centre-forward and that they had a left-winger called Gallego. I only remember his name because my mate, Quinn, who was a bit of a swot, wondered if he was related to the man who perfected the refracting telescope. I said I didn't know but thought it highly unlikely. Quinn went to Cambridge so he probably found out before I did.

Anyway, my mate Sippy Salt was the best closet winger I played with. It didn't matter if the closets were on his right or left-hand side, made of wood or brick. On song he was unstoppable and when I broke the goalscoring record of our street team with 163 goals in a season (the record still stands, unlike the closets) it was mainly due to the service provided by him.

If we are to be serious for a moment, the decline of the winger in British football is generally accepted as having commenced with the appointment of Sir h'Alf as England's team manager in the sixties. I think it started earlier than that with the introduction of inside toilets into houses in the north of England. The demolition of the outside closet was the death of the old-fashioned dribbler. It is well worth FIFA looking closely at this subject as they deliberate ways and means of making soccer in the future more attractive. It is, after all, only by looking at our history that we discover the future.

That being the case, let me offer one or two recollections of the past that might be of help to today's hard-pressed administrators. They must not believe that the problems they are facing in the modern game are either new or insurmountable. Indeed they are almost piffling compared to some of the problems we had to sort out in the Barnsley and District Backyard League. Our league was dominated for several seasons by a side skippered by a sociopath who wore a cloth cap which he would often remove to chastise his opponents with a good nebbing. (To neb: old Yorkshire pastime; to beat about the head with the furled peak of a cap.)

He neutered our closet wingers by removing the doors to the outside toilet on match days. But his most successful tactic was the use of his pet dog. This creature looked like a cross between a collie and an alligator and would bite anyone who came within five yards of its owner. If the side happened to be a couple of goals down a whistle would bring the dog on to the field whereupon its master would,

unchallenged, score the goals required for victory. We had to wait until the dog ran under a coal lorry before things changed. I offer that anecdote to FIFA only to show that if they think they've got problems they don't know they're born.

However, a practical suggestion for speeding up play concerns the way that modern players spend an inordinate amount of time rolling around in agony over some alleged foul when they ought to be on their feet running after a football which is what they are paid for in the first place. This is always a problem area for referees because assessing if the player is genuinely hurt or simply shamming is difficult.

A team I played for once solved this problem by employing a trainer whose infallible way of discovering if a player was really injured or not was to begin his examination by biting him on the neck. The sight of him running on to the field, fitting his false teeth as he approached, was enough to deter any malingerer.

Indeed I have seen men with shattered limbs attempt to struggle to their feet to escape his diagnosis. One of the problems about being bitten by him was you didn't know whose teeth he was wearing at the time. He would make a random selection from his sponge bag which was where he held his players' teeth in safe keeping. Again I am not suggesting that modern trainers go around biting their players but I do think there is enough evidence of its effectiveness as an antidote to a problem still with us to warrant further investigation by FIFA.

I hope they take my suggestions seriously in Zurich. I am hopeful. They might sound barmy but the people at FIFA are used to that. It was they, after all, who gave the next World Cup to the Yanks.

In the end, what they all agreed on was that Kenny Dalglish jacked it in because of pressure. It was 10 years ago that I expressed the heartfelt wish never again to hear the word "pressure" used about sport; since when I have aged 20 years under the pressure of hearing pressure become the most overused word in the entire sporting vocabulary.

My problem is that I can't for the life of me relate the word to athletic pursuits which, I always imagined, were designed to alleviate our worries, not add to them. Nor can I imagine why anyone who is paid to play sport should have a nervous breakdown about it.

The word "pressure" is often used to suggest that the modern athlete has an intolerable strain, imposed simply by competing. This is when I start thinking of words like tosh, balderdash, drivel, a heap of nonsense, not to mention a load of cobblers.

In my view, if we are to talk about the real world then pressure is something that nurses know about, or people who grind out a living in a factory or men who dig coal a mile underground. Pressure is being poor, or unemployed, or homeless or hopeless. What it's not is being paid £200,000 a year to manage one of the world's great football teams.

I am not blaming Kenny Dalglish for the excessive use of the word to explain his predicament. He's not a whinger nor inclined to self-pity. What I do find interesting and significant is that a man so embroiled in the game, so single-minded in his pursuit of excellence both as a player and a manager and successful in all his ambitions should become so disenchanted that he retired at the age of 39.

It's not as if he's taking time off to write a novel or back-pack through Patagonia or learn the saxophone. What he has done is the equivalent of switching off his life-support system. This tells you more about the game and what has happened to it than it does about the state of Kenny Dalglish's mind.

The main trouble is that no-one has any fun any more. Everyone is too po-faced about the game. It's all too tactical, too strategic for its own good. It used to accommodate the poets and the dreamers; the managers had the licence to be whimsical. Not any more.

When I was writing a book about George Best he told me that often when United had a team talk, Sir Matt Busby would tell him not to bother turning up. I checked with Sir Matt. "It wasn't worth him coming," he explained. "Why not?" I asked. "Well, it was a very simple team talk," he said. "All I used to say was: 'Whenever possible give the ball to George'."

Then there was the incomparable Bill Shankly giving his team talk about the aforesaid Manchester United side. He went through the opposition one by one saying: "He cannae play fitba" or "He is not fit to lace your boots". At the end he said to his men: "So there you are, lads, man for man we're far superior. They have nae chance. Any questions?" Tommy Smith said: "Yes, boss, you've not mentioned Best, Law and Charlton." Shankly became angry and shouted: "Are you tellin' me ye cannae beat a team with three men in it?"

When I first started watching football, the manager was a sombre and authoritative figure on a level with the local magistrate or the school headmaster. He wore a large overcoat and a trilby hat. He sat in the stand, and was always referred to as Mister.

Angus Seed put together the teams I cut my teeth on at Barnsley. He had a marvellous eye for a player. He spotted Tommy Taylor in a local team, paid Glentoran a few quid for an unknown called Danny Blanchflower. He gave a chance to a young Chilean called George Robledo, brought Johnny Kelly and Jimmy Baxter down from Scotland.

I have received a letter from Johnny Kelly's brother-in-law in Glasgow telling me my hero was celebrating his 71st birthday, that he was in good health, jogging every day and still playing football. May the sun rise on his shiny, bald head for many more years. I sent him a card: "To the hero of my youth."

Silly isn't it, a grown man hero-worshipping a player he last saw play 40 odd years ago? Yet when I think of him it seems like yesterday and I see him clearly taking up his place on the wing on the far side of the ground with the brewery and the pit in the background.

His partner was a truly remarkable inside-left called Jimmy Baxter. Nowadays they wouldn't let him on a soccer field – he would fail the medical. He was just over 5ft 6in tall and weighed 9½st. He had legs like pipe-cleaners and boots which seemed to turn up at the toes like skis. He had a lop-sided grin and a slightly gormless expression and looked like he had been reared on Woodbines and dripping sandwiches. Indeed, he was renowned for having a smoke at half-time and lighting up in the bath at the end of the game.

He was a marvellous player: tireless, for all his dedication to Woodbines, and tough, in spite of his physique. But mostly he was inventive, subtle and witty. He never made a fuss about controlling a ball, no matter what speed or angle it came to him, no matter how tight the marking.

Like all great players he made his own space and played at his chosen rhythm and in Kelly he found the perfect partner. Behind them, and on the other side of the park was Danny Blanchflower. It is true to say that until he came to Barnsley we had not seen his like in our defence. Traditionally, the players who defended the Barnsley goal were hard men who dissuaded the opposition from playing in their half by the simple method of rewarding their ambition with a good kicking.

They were blue-collar soccer players in hobnailed boots and flat caps. Blanchflower wore cap and gown. To begin with, he flabbergasted the fans; then he beguiled them. The trouble with Danny was he had the old-fashioned idea that training involved playing with a ball, whereas the Barnsley manager had a theory that too much practising with a football tired the players for the game on Saturday. He preferred them to play snooker. Never one to tolerate a ludicrous situation, Danny fell out with the management and was transferred to Aston Villa. The rest, as they say, is history.

I wouldn't want you to run away with the idea that all of Angus Seed's signings were like Baxter and Blanchflower, though he did well enough, generally speaking, to satisfy and keep the job for nearly 20 years. Indeed, some of his signings were celebrated in the local paper in verse. Of George Robledo, the Chilean who later went to Newcastle United, a fan wrote a poem entitled Robledo, The Red Shadow.

I used to be able to quote it at length. Nowadays I am struggling to recall a couple of verses but I seem to remember:

> "Swooping down upon the foe,
> The fearless shadow streaks,
> The crucial moment is near,
> The air is filled with shrieks.

"With desperation in their hearts:
They give a cry of pain,
Then, crash, the ball is in the net,
Robledo strikes again."

Forty years ago this was pretty stirring stuff. And unforgettable too, as I've just proved. However, it would have taken the talents of Edward Lear to capture the personality of some of Mr Seed's more eccentric signings. There was, for instance, the centre-half who, after three home games, had scored five own goals. Things became so bad that our centre-forward used to mark his own centre-half to stop him heading past his own goalkeeper. He only lasted half a season but when he left he was our top scorer with eight goals, six through his own net.

We were nonplussed on the terraces, until one day a stranger said: "I hear he's got a plate in his head." We all felt sorry for him after that, without quite understanding what was wrong with him.

The point is that in all those years of watching the comings and goings, the promotions and relegations, the heroes and the villains, no-one ever used the word "pressure". I can speak for the players, too, because the conspiracy between players and fans in those days was complete. They travelled to the ground on the same bus, relaxed in the same snooker hall, danced at the Cuban Ballroom.

So what happened? Well, the reason for Kenny Dalglish's disenchantment is what happened. Everything changed and not much of it for the better. Up in Glasgow, Johnny Kelly celebrates his 71st birthday happy in the knowledge he is still playing the game he loves. In Liverpool a man in the prime of life and at the peak of his career says he's had enough. One represents the past, the other the present. If you had a choice who would you want to represent the future?

M y summary of the FA Cup Final is that whoever designed the shorts worn by Tottenham Hotspur should be made to wear them. Had Tottenham lost they could have claimed bad design as a contributory factor.

It says much for the strength of character of Terry Venables' men that not only did they overcome the loss of Gascoigne and lack of faith shown by the bookies; not only did they triumph against a background of turmoil and uncertainty at the club; but their ultimate achievement was that they did what they did while looking complete prats.

I have to go back to my days with the fabulous Cody's Congs to recall a team dressed in such a ludicrous manner. Our excuse was necessity and not fashion. Our team manager at the time had a brother-in-law who worked for Cody's Circus. He provided us with T-shirts which had names and not numbers on the back.

In those days I played centre forward in honour of my great hero, Cec McCormack. In Cody's Congs I had 'Ramon The Dwarf' on my shirt instead of No 9. Similarly our inside right was 'Sheba And Her Pythons', our right winger 'Carlos The Fire Eater' and our centre half 'Griselda the Bearded Lady'.

Looking back, I can see that we were foreshadowing the eventual link between showbiz and soccer, although we didn't know it at the time. In fact, we only played one season in our circus kit before being banned by the League. Broke and unable to afford any other outfit, we then played a season in Fair Isle sweaters knitted by the manager's wife. We didn't win many matches but we sure lost a lot of weight.

That was a long time ago, many years before soccer became a branch of the fashion industry. In those days my heroes turned out in red shirts and white shorts. They had nothing on their shirts except the number on the back. They wore leather boots with big toe caps and red and white socks that bulged with padding.

It seemed as if each sock was stuffed with eight quire of Picture

Post magazine. The socks finished just below the knee, the baggy white shorts just above. All that was visible of the player's leg was the white knobble of the knee cap. It looked like a man wearing a chef's hat peering over a wall.

If, as a child in those days, you were bought the club outfit, it remained the same until you became a man. The only need for change was when you outgrew the uniform. Today the clubs change the design every year. They found out long ago that if you plug commercialism into hero worship you create a powerful and lucrative response.

It is a dangerous area, as Wembley and the cup final showed. Fashion and soccer form a quirky relationship. I don't know if the Spurs players had final approval of the design of their Wembley kit, but if they didn't they should insist on it in future and sack the person who decided this time around.

I won't even bother to discuss the shirt which was a hideous parody of the lovely simplicity of the traditional kit. I will concentrate instead on the shorts. The designer had decided that baggy shorts are back. Nothing wrong with that except he must approach his task bearing in mind the great tradition of baggy shorts in soccer and the part they played in the game's history. In other words he is not simply designing a garment to cover a player's legs, he is paying proper respect to the memory of Alex James, Stanley Matthews, Tommy Harmer and Jimmy Leadbetter.

In case you need some background on the last two I should tell you that Harmer was a Spurs player of such frail physique that on him a G-string would have looked like a pair of bloomers. He was a marvellous player. If footballers were magicians he would have been Merlin. Leadbetter was another who wore the baggy shorts with style. As I remember him, his shorts and his socks were so long that you never saw an inch of bare leg.

He played in Alf Ramsey's wonderful Ipswich side operating from a no-man's land wide on the left hand side of the park, from which position (alone and unsung until it was too late) he lobbed footballs on to the noble brows of Phillips and Crawford, who were put on earth to score goals.

Another man who wore the baggy shorts with distinction was Cec McCormack. He came to Barnsley in 1951 from a non-League club. He had wispy blond hair and looked like a tall jockey. He took some

getting used to. We were reared on strapping centre forwards designed to uproot goalposts and shoulder-charge 'keepers into the net. McCormack showed us a different way.

He had a body swerve which dumbfounded opponents; he was quick and two-footed. In his first seven games he scored 13 goals. By season's end he had scored 33. He was as moody and mysterious as the Great Wilson in *The Wizard*. There were those of us who believed that instead of spending his spare time playing snooker like the rest of the team, he lived in the hills above Holmfirth on a magic diet of wild berries and spring water. He was patient too, like all the great goalscorers he had the instincts of a predator. He would circle an opponent, lurking, awaiting a mistake. When he saw a moment's hesitation or lack of concentration he would strike. I remember him playing against John Charles when that great footballer was playing for Leeds.

There wasn't a better player in the world than Big John. He didn't give McCormack a sniff until late in the game when the centre forward nipped past him to score. It was probably the only time in the match that McCormack touched the ball. It seemed like an afterthought. Big John showed a lot of leg for those days. Ccc wore his shorts down to his knees. One up for the baggy shorts brigade.

As I say, when we talk baggy shorts we are not just discussing fashion. We are talking about the history of the game. On the evidence of what we saw at Wembley the designer had not done his homework. There is plenty of evidence to hand.

Eye-witnesses abound, many of whom still have their collections of *Topical Times* glossy black and white photographs showing heroes, long dead, standing with one foot on a proper leather football in the days when they were paid eight quid a week, top whack, to kick it.

What the evidence shows is that baggy shorts work best when made from sturdy material like sail cloth. Modern fabrics make the baggies droop in ridiculous fashion when they should stand proud and shapely. Ideally, with the wind behind him and in full flight, a player wearing baggy pants should resemble a bulging spinnaker. If the material flaps then the effect is totally lost and the player becomes risible rather than majestic.

There are no doubt good reasons why modern designers want to use new materials. That being so, might I suggest an amendment to the present design which would require baggy shorts incorporating a wire frame to give them the authentic shape. Devotees of the More-cambe and Wise Show will remember the late and very excellent Eric Morecambe wearing a pair of wire-framed tennis shorts to great effect.

But not even Mr Morecambe, who was a comic genius, could have come up with anything so daft as the white slash at the bottom of the Tottenham Hotspur shorts. This was what finally and conclusively took the outfit from the area of sporting equipment into the world of fancy dress. It made the players look as if their shirts were sticking out of their trouser bottoms. Thank God they won. Fancy losing looking like that. Even in victory I wished they had been more presentable.

In a way their costume summed up what has been happening to Tottenham Hotspur Football Club. It is what occurs when you try to turn a soccer club into a shopping mall. But basically it is what happens when you confuse fashion with tradition and fail to appreciate that one is merely decorative while the other is the very foundation upon which everything is built. Without it you are struggling.

Had Paul Gascoigne been a racehorse his odds would have lengthened when the punters saw him in the parade ring. On the pitch before the game he was sweating up alarmingly. His foul on Parker was grotesque in execution, horrific in intent. The illegal challenge leading to his self-inflicted injury was stupid, the punishment he suffered almost biblical.

The irony was that by showing the worst of himself he brought the best from his teammates. He will now be able to contemplate his future at leisure. He and his advisers need time to decide not so much where he ends up playing but the far more important question of the sort of player he wants to be.

At present, comparisons with Best and the other all-time greats are silly and I will tell you why. The mark of the truly great player is that he dominates a game by his skill and not by kicking his opponents. Moreover, the big occasion sharpens their reflexes, stimulates their skills.

It doesn't give them a red mist in the eyes. There is a video of Best and Law walking on to the field in front of 90,000 people and as they meet the wall of sound they turn to each other and laugh. Paul Gascoigne should watch that video. Then he might learn what it is to have the world at his feet rather than planted in an opponent's chest.

A reporter rang the other day to ask what I was doing when England won the World Cup. I told him I was watching television like the rest of the country. He didn't seem happy with the answer, as if expecting me to admit I had been dancing naked around the village with garlands in my hair.

He wanted to know what I had done when the Germans scored the equaliser in the last minute of the game. I told him I wasn't worried, that my money had been on our chaps all along. The truth is I didn't see it because my eyes were closed. More than that, I was in the bathroom at the time, sitting on the loo and praying to the great Walter Winterbottom In The Sky to let England win.

When I heard the roar I rushed into the room and asked my youngest son what had happened. He said "Grumphgurglewillypotty", which is what you get when you ask a two-year-old a tactical question about soccer.

I knew everything would be all right in extra-time because I saw the Queen turn to Sir Stanley Rous and ask, "What is happening?" when the players stayed on the pitch after 90 minutes. You can't fool our monarch. She knew something was up.

The reporter also wanted to know if I thought Geoff Hurst's first goal in extra-time – the one he knocked in off the crossbar – was a goal. Twenty-five years on and they are still arguing about it? I told him straight. "Fifty million Englishmen can't be wrong," I said.

The trouble with nostalgia is it makes you feel old. It is one thing to be aware that it is 25 years since we won the World Cup. It is quite another to take your mind back all that time and place the event in the context of your own life. Only then do you realise how long ago it was and how much the world has changed.

We had just come down from Manchester and were living in a flat near St John's Wood. I was reporting soccer and cricket for a Sunday newspaper and working on a new current affairs programme on BBC television called Twenty-Four Hours. My colleagues in the studio were Cliff Michelmore and Kenneth Allsop.

You could say I was playing in the First Division. Every Saturday I went to the football, mainly back north because that was where Manchester United played and, in those days, they were an eyeful. Best was demonstrating the upper limits of his skill, Charlton was proving that if you gave Pele equal billing, the other two greatest footballers in the world were both playing for Manchester United.

If that wasn't enough, the imagination of Law, Charlton and Best was stoked by Paddy Crerand's diligent prompting. And you wonder why I went north each week?

Mind you, it wasn't too shabby in London. Spurs had the likes of Alan Gilzean and Jimmy Greaves and at Craven Cottage Johnny Haynes was still lording it, still conducting his tutorials to a wonderful bunch of eccentrics.

To go to Craven Cottage was to laugh a lot. Most of the humour came from the disparity between Haynes's ambition and the performance of his team-mates. His relationship with Tosh Chamberlain was one of the great comic partnerships of all time. Tosh was much loved by the Fulham supporters, and quite rightly so. He was an honest toiler with a fearsome shot which brought him many spectacular goals.

Haynes was supremely gifted, a magnificent distributor of the ball. The trouble between them was due to Haynes's imagination and Chamberlain's lack of it. When his plans went awry Haynes would stand, hands on hips, looking to a distant planet to beam him up while Tosh would untangle himself from the corner flag or the third row of spectators behind the goals.

The best piece of goalkeeping I ever saw happened at Craven Cottage and it came from a back-pass by Tosh. He was doodling with the ball on the half-way line when he decided that he would have more space if he retreated towards his own goal.

There are two theories about what happened next. The first is that Tosh tried to pass back and overhit the ball, the second that he forgot which way he was facing and mistook Tony Macedo in the Fulham goal for the opposition keeper. In any event, he let rip from about 40 yards. Macedo, who wasn't expecting this to happen as he assumed Tosh was on his side, flung himself to his right and tipped the ball over the bar.

That was what it was like 25 years ago. It was fun and a bit silly.

The country was in a mess but the citizens didn't care. Mary Quant dictated the fashion, the Beatles wrote the music and Carnaby Street started in London and encircled the world.

It is important to understand what it was like in 1966 in order to comprehend how much Alf Ramsey was an alien figure in the landscape. He remains the most unlikely, incongruous icon of the 1960s. While the rest of the world went giddy, dressing like peacocks, Alf stuck to his demob suit. It was as if no-one told him that the war was over. I wrote at the time that he reminded me of a puritan at an orgy.

But, while the rest of us day-dreamed about winning the World Cup in style with wingers who could dribble and the likes of Greaves lurking in the box, Alf Ramsey had a plan. It wasn't pretty, but it was certainly effective. What he searched for were individuals who might have individual weaknesses yet, when placed together, represented a unit without fault.

When asked if he would pick George Best if that player had been an Englishman, Alf said he would have to think about it. He was not denying Best's genius, merely considering the possibility that in spite of all his gifts he might not fit the jigsaw.

Looking back at what I wrote at the time, I realise I could not have been more wrong about Ramsey and what he was trying to do. But I was not the only one. Soccer managers of today who think they are misunderstood by the media should refer back to the kind of press Ramsey used to get and think themselves blessed.

The mutual antipathy was inevitable when you consider Alf's dislike of the spotlight and our inability to understand what he was doing.

Importantly, the players felt differently about the boss. I made a film called *The Boys of '66* on the 20th anniversary of the victory and found a unanimous and heart-felt admiration for Ramsey from all his players.

He convinced them they were going to win the World Cup. "Don't worry about Brazil," he said when the rest of us had made them favourites. "Pretty amazing conclusion when you think about it," George Cohen told me, still smiling at the cast-iron certainty of his manager.

Cohen said if you played for Ramsey he made you feel part of an elite outfit. On the other hand, you could never find comfort in the thought that the manager regarded you as irreplaceable. Gordon

Banks, by common consent the greatest goalkeeper in the world at the time, said that after one game he bade farewell to the manager by saying: "I'll see you." The boss replied: "Will you?"

Bobby Charlton tells a story about being approached by the team to sort out a problem with Ramsey. They were going to play in a hot climate and the specially tailored grey suits for the trip were made of a heavy material.

Working on the principle that Charlton was the one player who could query Ramsey without getting an earful, the players delegated him to voice their complaint. Bobby told Ramsey of the problem, concluding: "So the lads thought maybe you could let us wear our blazer and flannels rather than the suit." Alf thought a moment and replied: "I have a completely open mind on the matter . . . tell them to wear the suits."

Alf and his team won the World Cup and became the most famous men in Britain. Bobby Moore got a gong and Alf was knighted. Not too long after, Sir Alf got the sack and Bobby Moore was managing Southend United. Whichever way you look at it, we are careless with our sporting heroes.

I saw Alan Ball the other day. He has a bar and restaurant near where I live. He was saying that the players were given £1,000 minus tax for winning the World Cup while the Football Association paid more than £1 million in tax from the profits they made.

Like the rest of them he is not bitter, more bemused by it all. For all his 70-odd caps, he is still known as the kid who ran the legs off the Germans in extra-time, part of the team who won the World Cup. That's the nice part of the story. The rest is measured out in anniversaries when people remember again what happened that July day in 1966.

What is missing after all these years is Alf Ramsey's account of events. Typically, he has said very little. He remained constant throughout success and failure, which is to say he revealed nothing of his true feelings. The nearest he came to verbosity was on the 20th anniversary when he told an interviewer: "The facts speak for themselves."

We were filming Bobby Charlton coaching a group of youngsters and he was telling them about winning the World Cup and how wonderful it was to understand you were the best in the world.

Their eyes were as large and bright as polished hub caps. Then one

said: "Please sir, my grandad used to watch you play when he was little." I don't know if it got to Bobby but it sure made me feel old. Mind you, he and the rest of the team have something over the rest of us. We were famous for 15 minutes. They are immortal.

L et us return to the fine wine. When I wrote about Don Davies I had no idea so many readers had been waiting 30 years or more to tell someone how much they appreciated his contribution to sports journalism.

A book published in 1963, called *Don Davies – An Old International* by Jack Cox, is both an appreciation of his life and a representation of some of his best writing. I do have a copy of the book. I bought it many years ago at a second-hand bookshop for sixpence and I treasure it.

Bill Bland, of Twickenham, wrote to say that I could copy his book but not borrow it. And if I wanted a photostat, it would have to be done in his 'manor' as he was never letting his copy out of his sight. I don't blame him. The book is impossible to obtain nowadays, underlining the need for a new, updated version, or, better still, a new compilation of Don Davies' work.

What I omitted to mention in my appreciation was that Davies also wrote beautifully about cricket. Actually, the man wrote beautifully about anything. I should imagine his letters of complaint to the Gas Board were works of art.

Albert Smale, the secretary of Little Lever Cricket Club in Lancashire, tells me that Davies was also an outstanding batsman with Bradshaw in the Bolton Association before 1930. He has produced his averages showing that in 1920 his figures were 18 innings, six not out, 114 not out his highest score with an average of 35.8. In 1921 he scored 625 runs in the season at an average of 36.7.

Marcus Harrison wrote to tell me that he can remember Davies striding to the wicket at Bradshaw in the Twenties. He writes: "He was always immaculate, not only sartorially but, even more importantly, in his behaviour on and off the field. He was an amateur in the fullest sense and I recall that he never accepted talent money when his graceful strokes produced the magical 50 as they often did. In elegance and 'joy-to-watch' terms, I would liken him to David Gower."

The only dissonant note was struck by a couple of correspondents who rather doubted Don Davies's report of the game where Iremonger, a goalkeeper of great eccentricity who played for Notts County, took a penalty kick, hit the crossbar, chased downfield in pursuit of the rebound and, in trying to clear his lines, scored a spectacular own goal.

I wasn't there, but having observed goalkeepers for most of my life I have no reason to doubt the accuracy of the report. Indeed, it would not have surprised me had Mr Davies recalled that at the time of the reported incident, Iremonger was wearing an ostrich feather in his cap and wheeling a pram. As Mr Davies often pointed out, it isn't necessary to have a slate loose to be a goalkeeper, but it certainly helps.

It enables us to understand the problems facing what used to be called "custodians" if we draw up a list of requirements for the job. To begin with, goalkeepers need the agility of a circus acrobat and the courage of a jump jockey. It helps if they have the metabolism of a polar bear, the diving ability of a seal and the nerve of a steeplejack. They must have the ability to take more stick than a seaside donkey and it definitely helps if there is madness in the family.

Strangely enough, some of the men who met those requirements and had long and successful careers between the posts were unlikely looking paragons. Chick Farr, who kept for the old, lamented Bradford Park Avenue just after the Second World War looked like a refugee from a Lowry dole queue. He wore the biggest cap I ever saw, with a peak so big it took the sun from his knees.

He was the first 'keeper I encountered who liked to venture outside his penalty area. He delighted in tackling an oncoming forward before charging upfield and demonstrating to his team-mates how to dribble. When you consider that his team at that time included the immortal Len Shackleton, you can see that Farr had cheek as well as daring.

His party piece was to pull down the crossbar when he either couldn't be bothered to jump for the ball or, more likely, judged that the shot might beat him. As I write, I can see Johnny Kelly cutting in from the left at Bradford and hitting a shot to win a Cup tie for Barnsley. I was out of my seat cheering as Farr reached up with both hands, pulled down the bar and allowed the ball to sail into the crowd.

What happened on those occasions was that the referee would deliver a stern lecture which Farr would listen to with his cap pulled down over his ears, making him look even more gormless.

The referee, unable to convince himself that anyone who looked so soppy could have an unworthy thought, would let him off with a lecture. What he didn't know was that under that huge cap lurked a criminal mastermind.

It often happens that goalkeepers have to throw themselves on the mercy of referees and the best ones become magnificent advocates. Some, like Farr, plead insanity. Others make use of their physical attributes, or lack of them. I once saw a match in Fiji where the goalkeeper for the national side was cross-eyed, not marginally so, but very cross-eyed in the manner of Ben Turpin.

You all remember Ben Turpin, don't you? His best silent film was the one where he played a boxer who laid out everyone in the ring, including the referee, because of his inability to see straight.

I particularly remember the film because when I saw it as a child, my father was asked to leave the cinema following numerous complaints that he was causing a disturbance with his hysterical laughter.

I thought of Turpin when I saw the Fijian 'keeper because when he went for a cross, no-one was safe in the penalty area. When the referee drew his attention to the opposition centre-forward lying bleeding in the goalmouth minus a few teeth, and asked him to explain why the teeth were embedded in his fist, the 'keeper was able to blame his poor eyesight and point out that his own centre-half was also in need of urgent medical attention having been mistaken for an onrushing forward.

It was sufficient to keep him on the field and to ensure that for the rest of the match, he was able to do his job unhindered by either friend or foe.

I suppose the best goalkeeping eccentric I ever saw was Sam Bartram. Sam liked the odd gallop downfield and no-one ruled his box like he did. He hated forwards, particularly those who tried to take the mickey out of him.

I remember one game at Barnsley during the War when he was guesting for York City and we were awarded a penalty. I think Beaumont Asquith took the kick. It was a fancy name for a Barnsley lad, but it served him well when he retired and became a milkman. "Who delivers your milk?" "The Co-op as a matter of fact." "Who delivers yours, as if it matters?" "Beaumont Asquith, that's who."

He was a studious soccer player who delighted in sending the 'keeper the wrong way from the penalty spot. He did it to Bartram.

He wiggled his hips, Sam dived right and Asquith rolled the ball into the opposite corner. Whereupon Sam retrieved the ball and kicked it over the grandstand and into the street.

In those days, footballs were in short supply. One had to last a season. Play was held up while a search party was organised to find the ball during which time Bartram was able to advise Asquith that any repeat of the trick might result in him taking a trip over the stand instead of the ball.

To see a great goalkeeper in action is to be reminded of the old definition of style as being grace under pressure. Of the moderns, Gordon Banks, Peter Shilton and Pat Jennings stand out. Both were dictators of their domain, challenging anyone to behave badly on their patch. They were able to make the difficult look commonplace but, at the same time, to defy the imagination with their anticipation and their athleticism.

There were two in my youth I particularly admired. Both played for Manchester City. One was Frank Swift and the other Bert Trautmann. If you liken soccer players to cricketers then Trautmann was Tom Graveney and Swift was Fred Trueman in his pomp. Like Graveney, Trautmann was incapable of an awkward movement. Everything he did, even flicking back his hair or tying a bootlace, was done as if set to music.

He was given ample chance to demonstrate his talents because the City defence in those days would have given the modern coach a severe attack of the vapours. It was, however, wonderful to watch. It seemed like the team consisted of Bert Trautmann in goal with 10 forwards making up the rest. Trautmann was all they needed. He was graceful and brave and commanded such respect and adoration that any forward who had the audacity to score against him at Maine Road must have felt like going behind the goal and apologising to Bert's fan club.

Big Swifty, like F S Trueman, was a palpable star. Once he took the field it was impossible to watch anyone else. The first time I saw him, he came to Barnsley in a Cup tie and demonstrated the art of goalkeeping.

He loved showing off. I remember him catching the ball one-handed like a man picking apples and then holding it above the head of a Barnsley forward called Gavin Smith. Every time Smith jumped to try and get to the ball Swift would wait until his brow was near the ball

and then lift it tantalisingly out of reach. He was like a man teasing a dog with a bone.

Frank Swift died along with most of the Manchester United team in the Munich air crash of 1958. So did Don Davies. The measure of both men is that, more than 30 years on, we remember them and in doing so smile with pleasure and in gratitude.

Further proof that the people who are in charge of the new Premier League don't live in the real world came with the announcement that the chairman of a bank will head up the organisation. This was seen by the organisers as something of a coup, whereas in the snug of the Rat and Handbag the lads were saying that a bank manager was the last person they would choose to represent either popular support or financial credibility.

On the other hand, if the Premier League is to be the cock-up it promises, then who better to have in charge than someone from an industry which thought the late owner of Oxford United was a man you could lend money to.

But the biggest problem soccer faces, much more difficult than the number of teams in the new league or the quality of grounds, is how to produce the footballers to justify the revolution. What will be needed, more than ever, are stars; players who can fill stadiums and restore some confidence and pride to our game.

What's required is a bit of swank and swagger. I am not advocating loudmouthed immodesty, but the kind of justifiable confidence which would lead to Sir Garfield Sobers looking out of his window early in the morning and saying: "I'd hate to have to bowl at me today."

You'd know what I mean if ever you saw Best and Law strut the field when United were in their pomp or Souness lord it when Liverpool were winning everything in sight. It's what Strachan gives to Leeds and Robson to the present United. But it's a rare commodity nowadays.

From what I've seen, modern teams lack conductors, players who dictate the rhythm and the tempo of play. The average soccer match today starts at 100 mph and only slows down through exhaustion. It has the athletic ambition and the spectator appeal of a hamster on a treadmill. If that had been the soccer of my youth I would never have bothered with the game, dismissing it for its lack of variety, imagination and, above all, beauty. It was the playmakers of my youth – the

Shackletons, the Mannions, the Carters, the Hayneses – who whetted the appetite and demonstrated the infinite possibilities.

They were what used to be called inside forwards. They were always a cut above the rest. To start with they seemed more intelligent than most of their team-mates. They carried with them an air of intellectual superiority, sometimes even allowing themselves slight eccentricity of style – shirt outside shorts in the Corinthian (slightly foppish?) manner, hair much longer than was deemed necessary or indeed manly in those days.

We had one at Barnsley called Roy Cooling, blond and handsome. In those days I was much affected by American writers. I wrote that Cooling looked like Scott Fitzgerald. It came out in the paper that he resembled Scott of the Antarctic. When I asked my boss for an explanation he said no-one in Barnsley had heard of Scott Fitzgerald but everyone knew who the other Scott was.

Visiting inside forwards were to be feared as much as enjoyed. They were the ones who could do terrible things to your team while making you wish that you could watch them every week.

I only watched Len Shackleton four or five times, but I can see him clearly now against the hazy background of a thousand forgotten games and players. He was one of the greatest entertainers our game has ever produced.

He illuminated the dark, drab days of post-war Britain. He gave the vast crowds who came to see him something to remember and to dream about. When modern techniques of close control are debated as if they are something new, I remember Shackleton taking the ball from any angle, at any speed and taming it in an instant.

His control was so sudden and subtle that you didn't realise what he was doing. He didn't trap a ball, he hypnotised it.

If he was the Cavalier of those times, Raich Carter was the Roundhead. Carter didn't run out of the tunnel on to the pitch, he would arrive in his own time at his own pace like a judge opening the local Assizes.

He looked magisterial, his hair slicked down and precisely parted, his tread measured and authoritative. I first saw him play for Sunderland at Barnsley. He walked on to the pitch some time after his teammates, looked around the field with a great show of disdain, and then meandered through the game until he decided it was time to put an end to proceedings.

He was 30 yards from our goal with his back to it when he took a wild waist-high pass on his right instep, killed it, flicked it to the ground, spun and without looking up, hit a left foot shot into the top corner of our net. He didn't pause to see where the ball went. He knew. He continued his full turn and walked to the centre spot. That night he went into my world team to play Mars and I composed a special prayer that Mr Carter might marry a Barnsley girl and come and play for us.

As it was he ended up at Hull City where he took all the free kicks, corners, penalties and throw-ins as part of this weekly demonstration that any team with Raich Carter in it didn't need anyone else to get a result.

A bit of that is what is needed now. We require someone to put the foot on the ball and have a look around. Any scheme for the future of soccer must take into account the quality of the product. At present it's not very good, and it's significant that the discussions so far about the game's future have involved directors of clubs but not the players.

Perhaps the FA are working on the theory that directors are the ones that count and not the players. Don't laugh. It's not a new thought. Many years ago the aforesaid Len Shackleton wrote a book about soccer. In it he included a chapter headed: 'What The Average Soccer Director Knows About The Game'. There followed a couple of blank pages. That was more than 30 years ago.

It is a clear sign that an election is getting tight when politicians start taking sport seriously. Both main parties have now declared that they would review the recommendations in the Taylor Report that soccer grounds become all seated.

Mr Hattersley said that the next Labour Sports Minister would review the matter urgently. He added that the Minister might be a woman.

Soccer fans wouldn't mind if the job was given to a hermaphrodite, provided it had a place in the Cabinet, an important voice in decision-taking and an avowed policy to improve sport in Britain, not just soccer but across the board.

What we will end up with, no matter who wins, is a Minister for Sport who sits some distance from the corridors of power, who will likely be attached to some other ministry like Agriculture and Fisheries (file 'Sport' under 'Codswallop') and who will spend a parliamentary career powerless, penniless and potless.

Am I being unduly cynical? Not a bit of it. I am merely reporting on the fate to have befallen every other Minister for Sport you can care to mention which is one of the reasons why we are still debating the kind of football stadiums we should have for the future when every other country besides Botswana and the Cocos Islands have already built theirs.

The present concern for sport as polling day approaches is typical of how politicians are adept at using the subject for short-term gain while ignoring its long-term problems. For instance, it would be wrong to reconsider the Taylor Report because some fans say they prefer to stand at football matches and there is a likelihood that less wealthy clubs will be forced out of business.

We should never forget why Lord Taylor was called upon to make his report. I had thought that the ghastly images of that awful day had been burned forever in the minds of anyone who saw them. Apparently not.

Sadly, because the people who run soccer are incapable of seeing further than the next television contract, the real purpose of the Taylor Report is reduced to an argument about whether or not spectators should stand or be seated.

What the Taylor Report offered was a chance for everyone concerned in soccer – officials, players, spectators, politicians even – to sit down and create a blueprint for the game for the next 100 years.

Anyone who comes to that debate mithering about standing up instead of sitting down or worried about the fate of Aldershot Football Club should be excluded on the grounds that he has not yet understood the difference between the future and tomorrow.

I am allowed a say on this question of standing up at football matches because I first planted my feet on the terraces at Barnsley when I was five and spent the next 15 years or more rooted to the spot. My position changed according to my rate of growth.

For the first few years I rested my chin on the concrete wall separating the spectators from the players and saw many wondrous things. We had a centre-forward called Kitchen who specialised in sliding tackles designed to take the winger and the ball into touch.

They were spectacular efforts often launched some distance from the target, who would be dillying and dallying with his foot on the ball when, suddenly and without warning, he would end up in a twisted heap at the bottom of our wall amid a terrible noise of stud on bone.

Kitchen rarely missed. He was like a heat-seeking missile. Once locked on to his subject, they were doomed. There were those who swore that Kitchen had so perfected his technique that midway through his sliding tackle he could swerve around obstacles, like teammates, who got in the way.

I can't confirm that but I do remember the one occasion that he missed his target. The winger jumped at the last minute and Kitchen slid underneath him like a runaway bull and hit the concrete wall full on. The damage was considerable, with concrete chips flying in all directions. The result was so spectacular that those of us in the front line who were showered with debris turned up at future games wearing motorbike goggles to protect our eyes and in honour of our hero.

What visiting wingers who had to patrol our touchline made of us, I don't know. Not that they expected anything other than a hard time when they visited Barnsley.

One of Mr Kitchen's victims was stretched on the turf awaiting urgent medical attention when he heard one of the Barnsley supporters shout at the trainer: "Don't revive him. Bury the sod."

Similarly, the chorus from the terraces whenever a member of the opposition was hit in the unmentionables and was being approached by the trainer with magic sponge and slopping bucket, was: "Nay lad, don't wash 'em. Count 'em."

In those days trainers looked like window cleaners and the likelihood was that when they weren't looking after players on a Saturday afternoon, they might well shine windows for a living.

Similarly, the winger you cheered so lustily on Saturday afternoon might well be working alongside you down the pit on Monday morning.

If you waited long enough after a game at Oakwell, you could travel home on the same bus as your hero. In those days there was a proximity between fans and players, a relationship betwixt the community and the club.

All that changed, as inevitably it had to, but it was lovely and warm and fulfilling while it lasted. (What it also meant was that a player's misdemeanours went no further than the family circle.)

This was demonstrated one Christmas in the days when the festive season meant three games in four days and an often unsuccessful attempt by some players to mix the Christmas spirit and a packed League programme.

One such miscalculation by one of our full-backs saw him on Boxing Day place the ball for a free kick and then walk unsteadily backwards until his knees hit our wall whereupon he buckled backwards into the crowd on the terraces.

His head came to rest near my feet. He looked very peaceful and his eyes were closed but he smelled like the tap room at our local pub. The trainer came bobbing up "Leave him there. Let him sleep it off," said Girt Jim.

There was Jim, Louis, my dad and three or four others who stood for 20 years or more on the terraces at Barnsley. I used to pray I would grow quickly so I would be allowed to join them. When I was 12 or 13 I was sent to bed for a month with some adolescent disorder. When I arose I had grown a foot.

"Up here with us," is what they said when they saw me next. I had arrived. And here, standing on a level with the men, I had a different view from the terraces, and learned much that was useful later on by just listening.

Those were the days before the songs of support and the concerted chanting.

This was the time when the lone and often despairing voice of dissent was heard from the terraces. Brentford were playing at Barnsley one day and had in their ranks a full-back called Gorman. He was a good player but bald as a coot.

It was a sunny day and Gorman's head was glistening in the sun. He went to head a ball and it slid from his pate for a throw-in. "Tha' wants to put some bloody chalk on it Gorman," said a man standing near to us.

Alf Ramsey, already an England player and calm as a judge, came to Barnsley with an unsullied reputation. Johnny Kelly turned him inside out, dizzied him, nutmegged him, played with him like a yo-yo and when Ramsey finally collapsed in the mud as Kelly cut inside him, a voice on the terraces said: "Ramsey, tha'rt about as much use as a chocolate teapot."

Those were the days when fans of both teams were allowed to stand together and there was intelligent competition for the observation of the day. The standard was high and excluded foul language.

My all-time favourite remark was made by a visiting Chesterfield supporter who watched silently as his team prepared to take a penalty in the dying seconds of a game at Barnsley which would have given them the draw.

In those days, games between Chesterfield and Barnsley were always keenly fought when Chesterfield had defenders like Ray Middleton in goal, Kidd and Milburn, as formidable and frightening a pair of full-backs as ever kicked a winger, and forwards of the quality and class of Linacre and Capel.

Capel was the captain on this day and he ordered up his brother to take the important penalty kick. The unfortunate Capel Junior made a terrible hash of things and belted the ball yards over the bar. As the ball disappeared into the Kop the Chesterfield fan said, to no-one in particular: "Nepotism. Bloody nepotism."

It was greeted in silence because no-one understood what he had said. It was only when I got home and looked up the dictionary that I realised what a gem it had been.

But all that changed long ago and it's no good yearning for what's

disappeared. Lord Taylor wasn't required to change the game I grew up with. He had to deal with what it had become; out of date, out of touch and dangerous.

The next step is the most important that the game has taken since the formation of the present League system. The most difficult job will be to rehouse and reshape soccer while remembering just who it really belongs to.

We, who grew up on the terraces, had it by right. The big question is – can it be given back by design?

My plan was to step from the plane and take a bob or two from my friends at golf. My theory was that I would be loosened by the Australian sun while they would be cramped by winter. Moreover, I had played most days for the past five or six weeks while they, most likely, had been restricted to the odd outing.

Mind you, my confidence had received a severe jolt a few days before I departed Australia when I played a round with Richie Benaud Mr Benaud, a respectable nine handicapper, had sponsored my application for membership of a Sydney club and had suggested playing in the midweek competition before we paraded in front of the committee, wearing our best suits, for the interview.

We made up a fourball with two very pleasant members who were strangers to me but known to Mr Benaud, and set off upon our round. Now, I don't know about you, but I am sometimes overcome by a strange affliction on a golf course – I cannot hit the ball properly. Most times I can give quite a passable imitation of a golfer. Now and again it can appear as if I have never been on a course in my life.

Fortunately Mr Benaud is a patient man. Moreover, being an experienced broadcaster, he knows when words are superfluous. Generally speaking, most of my round defied comment.

This did not prevent me from loudly criticising my own performance. Have you noticed that whenever golfers play badly the first thing that happens is their swing quickens and then they start talking to themselves?

I refrained from throwing my clubs. I only do that nowadays when I am playing with the wife and then it is her clubs I throw in a feeble attempt to win now and again. Nor did I curse. But I did question what on earth I was doing wasting my time on a golf course when I could be doing something constructive with my life, like leaping from the highest part of the Sydney Harbour Bridge.

I was saying this to a tree on the ninth hole when one of our opponents approached. "Relax" he said "It's only a game".

"You are right, I suppose it could be worse?" I said.

"How so?" he asked, thinking I was talking about golf, and sounding concerned.

So I told him about the impending interview with the committee to finalise my application for membership.

"It's a good job none of them saw me today, otherwise they would be convinced I can't play the game" I said.

"I have to tell you" said my opponent. "That I am the chairman of the committee and very much look forward to seeing you at five o'clock".

I approached my partner. "Do you know who that man is?" I said. Mr Benaud nodded.

"Then why on earth didn't you tell me when we started?" I asked.

"I thought it might have a bad effect on your game" he said.

In spite of this traumatic experience I was in confident mood upon my return to England. I thought I might go out and murder a course so I rang my friend Lozza to play Temple. I should say that when I left Sydney it was 37 degrees and when I arrived home it was freezing. I, therefore, prepared for the new conditions with the thoroughness of an Arctic explorer.

First a pair of thick tights, then the long johns much favoured by Gabby Hayes in various westerns of my youth. Then a pair of long woollen socks, such as are advertised as once having been worn by German U-Boat commanders.

Up top I favoured a long sleeved thermal vest under a thick polo-neck sweater like Jack Hawkins wore in *The Cruel Sea*. Over this I wore a sleeveless quilted jacket, so I looked like a duvet with arms.

I protected my head with a balaclava and a pair of fur ear muffs and wrapped my fingers around carbon warmers before immersing my hands in fur lined mittens. I might not have looked sexy but all I can say is that, had Captain Oates been as careful, he would most certainly have returned. It was then that the phone went. It was Lozza to say the course was closed.

I said: "Groofudgurtogof".

He said: "Try taking your balaclava off before you speak". I had been away too long.

As it had taken me at least an hour to get dressed, I was determined to play. So I went down to the golf range and tried to hit balls into the whirling snow. After 15 minutes of trying to turn and swing in

my survival gear I came to the conclusion that it was an impossible ambition, like ballroom dancing in a space suit. What is more my eyes were leaking, my nose was running and my fingers looked like parsnips.

It was then I came to two important conclusions about life. The first is that modern travel enables you to make an ass of yourself in both hemispheres in the space of 36 hours. Second, and more importantly, I now realise the older I get the more I understand that sporting ambition is the banana skin of middle age.

L et me own up; I have a shady background for someone writing an article in praise of golf.

Once upon a time (and not too long ago) I was the founder and president of the Anti-Golf Society. This organisation was born out of my isolation as friend after friend succumbed to the game and spent hours on the golf course when they should have been doing something constructive, like joining me at the boozer, or going racing.

My society flourished for a while, particularly in Spain where I recruited several frustrated wives who didn't realise until too late that the Costa del Sol is the name of a golf course stretching from Malaga airport to Gibraltar.

Our most effective moment as a society occurred in Marbella when I presented for the first and only time the Anti-Golf Society's Award for The Worst Golfing Experience Of The Week. This was won by a gentleman from Basildon who took 125 shots to complete his round, including a spectacular 15 on a par-three when he had some trouble with a bunker.

There were similar hard-luck stories, but what made him a clear winner was that upon returning to the hotel he discovered his wife had run away with a Spanish crimper. Sadly he was not able to be present to receive his trophy because he was laid up in hospital with a broken leg, sustained after a fall from a stool in the bar while celebrating his appalling misfortune.

It was in Spain that my reluctant conversion to golf began. My teacher was Mr James Tarbuck, a passionate advocate of the game and a very fine player. Firstly he invited me to walk with him while he played a match against Mr Norman Hunter, the soccer player.

Those fortunate to have watched Mr Hunter play soccer will know that he did not take prisoners.

Sadly, he was born before his time, for he was surely put on earth to sort out the likes of Maradona. The 'Hand of God' would have counted nothing when it came up against 'God's Clog'.

The power of Mr Hunter's left peg was in evidence on the golf course when, after missing a short putt on the 18th and losing to Mr Tarbuck, he gave his putter a ferocious kick. As it spiralled spectacularly skywards, glinting in the Iberian sun, Mr Tarbuck said to him: "Norman, the caddie has just recognised you."

Shortly after this, Mr Tarbuck arranged my inaugural round. At the third hole he suggested I drive first and showed me the line. The shot looked difficult and dangerous because it involved driving over the top of a group of workmen. "Shout fore," said Mr Tarbuck. I did and was perturbed to see the men return my warning with what I took to be offensive gestures. "Tell them to sod off," said my friend. So I did and they retreated, shaking their fists.

I settled down and hit the shot in the direction specified by my partner. I looked to him for praise. "Good shot," he said, "except that the hole is down there", pointing in the opposite direction.

The most humiliating part was retrieving my ball watched by the workmen I had so abused and who were not used to seeing their course played back to front.

That I survived the ordeal and have arrived at my present state where I have dedicated my remaining years to the search for the perfect swing is a clear indication of golf's allure.

I am now a regular on the pro-celebrity circuit, where I am known as 'Awesome' Parkinson. This identity was bestowed upon me by Roger Davis during a round we played together some time ago. Mr Davis chose the word carefully after observing my game for several holes. What convinced him was an eight-iron to the green which he suggested I should float on the breeze. What happened was I thinned the shot and the ball nearly knee-capped a spectator, took the top from a grassy knoll, hit a tree and came to rest four feet from the flag. Mr Davis regarded the carnage and shook his head. "Awesome", is what he said, and that is what I am called.

Pro-celebrity golf divides opinion. There are those who believe it is worth any amount of public humiliation just for the joy of playing a round with a great golfer. These are called Celebrities. Then there are those who take part only because they have to and who spend the entire round trying to avoid contact with their partner's swing just in case it is contagious. These are called Professionals.

The fact is that any joy there might be in a pro-celebrity game belongs exclusively to those of us who are lucky enough to march down the fairway with our heroes and pretend it is the last day of the Open and all we need is a birdie to take the trophy.

I have indulged that particular fantasy with the likes of Nick Faldo, Gary Player, Lee Trevino, Ronan Rafferty, Tony Jacklin, Neil Coles, Howard Clark, Roger Davis, Peter Senior, Ian Baker-Finch, to mention but a few.

All you learn is that you will never hit the ball like them even if you lived to be a hundred. What you envy is their rhythm, what you admire is their respect for the etiquette of the game and their patience with the hackers.

More than any other group of sportsmen, professional golfers are continually pestered by amateurs in search of a cure for a hook or a slice or, worst of all (and don't even say it, just spell it out) a s-h-a-n-k.

My approach is a little more subtle. I let them drink in my swing until they feel obliged to comment. They always do and none of it has been complimentary.

In the very first pro-celebrity I played in there were 2,000 people present to witness my drive from the first tee which went all of six inches and drew the observation from my partner, Neil Coles: "At least it went towards the hole."

I smashed my second shot into some trees on the left and was alone with my misery and about to play a wedge back on to the fairway when a voice said: "Excuse me."

I stopped at the top of my back swing and turned to see a man dressed in a long brown mac, carrying two plastic bags, standing behind me.

"Can I help you?" I asked, in amiable fashion.

"They're waiting for you on the green," he said.

"I know that," I said.

He looked at the club in my hand. "You won't get there with that," he said.

"Why don't you get lost," I suggested.

"I'll report you to the PGA," he said.

"How will you be able to talk with a pitching wedge in your mouth?" I enquired.

From that point on he followed me around the golf course, sometimes standing in my line on the fairway as I lined up a shot, always staring in silent retribution.

I told Mr Coles of my problem and sought his advice. "I'm

frightened of hitting him with the golf ball. How shall I avoid him?" I asked.

Mr Coles thought for a moment and then came up with the solution: "Aim at him," he said.

My final thought before I retire from the human race for four days to watch the Open is that I want whoever wins the Open to be someone I have played with.

This will confirm what I have always suspected: that the Good Lord plays off 16 and rewards those who are kind to hackers.

Whenever anyone asks me how I became interested in golf I blame the wife. She showed me how.

Her enthusiasms were intoxicating, her powers of persuasion overwhelming. How else can I explain my conversion from President of the Anti-Golf Society to confirmed addict? There was a struggle.

For a short period of time I became a Slob Golfer. This involved a reluctant interest in the game best defined as a cut-price protest. I played golf, but I refused to be seduced by its merchandising.

Thus I found a disgraceful bag and filled it with rusty clubs and secondhand balls. I played in a pair of modified cricket boots, old corduroys and a flat cap someone left at our house years ago. This ludicrous protest came to an end when, while playing my wife, I was approached by a man walking his dog on the course.

He watched Mary tee off and said: "That's a lovely swing." I agreed. He looked me up and down. "You her caddy?" he inquired.

Nowadays what you see when I step from the clubhouse is someone who blends into the golfing landscape, a man born to stride the fairways with a fair degree of confidence and style. This transformation is almost entirely due to the wife.

I wanted to be as happy as she is on a golf course and though I will never reach that state of nirvana, I am now at a stage where, generally speaking, the game improves my humour instead of ruining it.

I have a theory that women enjoy golf best of all because they see it primarily as a soothing pastime, whereas men mostly regard it as a test of aggression and strength. The fact is golf requires more of what are regarded as feminine qualities than almost any other sport I can think of.

It is a game requiring hands that are "soft", swings that are smooth. It best responds to gentle rhythms. It is about persuasion rather than power. It better suits the subtle patience of women than the brusque temperament of men.

You will realise, I hope, that I have just defined the difference

46

between me and the wife. It took me some time to realise that it was because of those differences that she was the better golfer. Perhaps men are also more stupid than women?

How else can I explain the times I tried to blast the ball from the tee instead of following her example of a relaxed and easy swing? Why did I take a three iron and end up in the water when she had already showed me that a five iron, a wedge and a putt was the sensible way to play the hole?

Why did I throw clubs and curse and grind my teeth while she would dismiss disappointment with a shrug of the shoulders? Why did she look at me piteously when I wanted to abuse the slow four-ball ahead or fight the galloping two-ball for driving into us?

Why is she a better golfer than I am? See above. The problem is getting rid of all those years of male conditioning. The frustrations men suffer on a golf course are not because they are playing badly but because they cannot solve problems with brute strength. I have been fortunate in that my two golfing mentors have been Mary and Lozza, a piano player by profession, who knows all about what I would call the adagio approach to golf.

It was Lozza who taught me the musical accompaniment to the golf swing designed to give it the correct speed and rhythm. This involves swinging the club to the opening bars of "The Blue Danube".

If you imagine the music as "Da, dee, da, daaa . . . dum" then the club should be taken back to "Da, dee, da". By the next "Daaa" it should be at the top of the backswing and starting the descent and the final "Dum" is the club head striking the ball and the follow through.

It works. Or at least it sets the swing to waltz time which, when you think about it, is about right. Try it. Humming is perfectly acceptable if you are unable to play the tune in your head. Whistling is not recommended because it sounds common and interferes with your breathing.

Other musical tips include using the song "Blue Moon" as an aid to putting. If you sing the first two words of the song as a ballad and take the putter head back on "Blue" and through on "Moon" you will do wonders for your game. If you need further guidance as to the correct tempo then I suggest Ella Fitzgerald's version on "The Rodgers and Hart Songbook" has it about right whereas Sinatra's on "Swingin' Session" is not quite right, despite having the better title for a golfer seeking inspiration.

Similarly both Lozza and I are convinced that the correct choice of music as you drive to the club is as important a part of preparation as half an hour spent chipping and putting. I find Johnny Hodges playing the blues and Ben Webster at his most languid ideal for the purpose.

The worst I ever saw Lozza play was when he arrived in a car driven by a friend who played a tape of "The Flight of The Bumble Bee" performed on a xylophone.

At no time are the soothing effects of music needed more than when a man plays his wife. People flogging pension funds and retirement villas in Portugal paint an idyllic picture of you and the missus spending a golden twilight together, walking down life's fairway towards the Great Clubhouse In The Sky. The message is that having worked together for so long you can now relax and see out the rest of your life as golfing partners.

I don't know what the figures are but my guess would be that this kind of selling has led to a sharp increase in the divorce rate among the over-60s. I recommend any couple thinking of getting married to play a round of golf together first. Unlike sleeping together before marriage, a pre-nuptial round of golf will give the woman the clearest indication possible of what life with him will really be like.

It takes a great deal of patience, fortitude, good humour and forgiveness if a married couple are to become golfing partners. There are fundamental differences and they must be addressed.

Take, for instance, the bag. In the main, women (meaning my wife) prepare their golf bag bearing in mind the possibility that while they are playing the 14th hole World War III will be declared and we will spend at least 12 months living in a bunker.

Therefore, in addition to a full set of clubs, my wife's bag contains a survival kit of sweets and various nibbles, a flask of tea, bottles of mineral water, insect repellants, sun creams and a tin of elastoplast. She will also have packed various articles of tropical clothing as well as thermal underwear, thick sweaters and a complete set of waterproofs in case she has to be rescued by the Felixstowe lifeboat.

I am nowhere near as organised, or prepared. My problem is that my sons nick my golf equipment and I have to take what's left.

What is funny is when we go to play Charity Pro-Ams together and the caddies see us coming. They jostle for Mary's attention figuring she'll have the smaller carry. They can't believe what they see when I point her bag out to them.

She loves pro-ams whereas I approach them as I would a rabid dog. The problem is they always play Mary in front of me so that throughout my round I am constantly being informed that the hole I just three-putted was birdied by my wife 15 minutes before.

It is even worse when they put us together in the same match. Pros love playing with Mary because she's always on the cut stuff and using her shots to get pars while they shoot for the birdies. Playing with me is a bit like going on a wildlife safari.

Moreover, when they look at her set-up and her swing they realise they have something to work with if she seeks advice. By comparison I represent a lost cause.

Once we played at Turnberry with Gary Player and his wife. We swapped partners for the encounter, Mary went into one of these impossible pot bunkers and couldn't get out. Mr Player showed her how and she hit the ball to within two feet of the pin.

Soon after I went into a similar bunker. I looked around for help. My three playing partners were looking out to sea. They thought they were being kind.

If we were to tally up the many games we have played against each other I would guess that the wife holds a substantial lead. However, there are signs that I am catching up.

It's not simply that I'm becoming a more canny golfer so much as I've learned to understand that defeat doesn't mean I have lost to a mere woman, rather I have been beaten by a better golfer.

I will not pretend our golfing relationship is perfect. It is generally true that if you see us walking together down the fairway you can assume that I am in the lead whereas if you see me trailing five yards behind looking hang-dog it's a fair chance I am three down with four to play.

There are still moments when defeat is hard to accept without rancour. Like the other day when she rolled one in from 15 ft to win on the last. I was choked and she knew it. She picked the ball from the hole and said, sweetly: "You know, there are times when I'd hate to be playing against me."

I am still trying to compose the musical antidote to that one.

The date of my full conversion to Golf As A Way Of Life can be put down to an event in Harrogate. It was on the outskirts of that noble spa at Pannal Golf Club that a tournament was held in my name. Now, I am the first to admit that the Michael Parkinson Golf Classic is a bit short on the kind of glitter surrounding a tournament named after Arnold Palmer or Seve Ballesteros, and certainly it's a long way removed from being the British Open. But give it time.

There are one or two things we learned from our attempt to create a significant new event in the sporting calendar. For one thing, in future, we must be more careful with our advertising. What I mean is we mustn't allow what happened on Friday, when the wind tore away the canvas sign causing it to flap backwards and the tournament to be renamed "CISSALC FLOG NOSNIKRAP LEAHCIM EHT". This sort of thing can upset the sponsors.

I wish I could report that I fought my way to the first tee through crowds of well-wishers. In fact, the only noise was the sound of the rain on my wet suit and the wind whistling up my trouser leg. I turned for a departing look at the club house as I embarked on the most important round of golf of my life and all I saw were a few faces at the rain-streaked windows looking forlornly out like holiday children confined to their boarding house.

My next contact with a member of the human race came at the third, where we came across a man carrying binoculars. I went out of my way to congratulate him for being our only spectator and to comment upon his fortitude. He looked at me as if I were barmy. "I haven't come for the golf," he said "I'm a birdwatcher."

I was reminded of the time I played in a similar tournament at Moor Park a few years ago, when it rained all day and we trudged the course like bedraggled survivors of some terrible disaster. Eventually I happened across a very well-known pop star driving a buggy. As he was a young man, and buggies in England are generally only issued on evidence of a doctor's note, I inquired as to his health. "Why do you ask?" he said. "Well, I thought you might have injured yourself which would explain the buggy," I answered. "I always take a buggy to showbiz events like this," he said. "Why?" I asked. "So I can escape from my fans," he said.

I looked around the surrounding countryside. We were alone on a storm-tossed hill. To the west, Bushey was lost in a deep depression, Rickmansworth was deserted and lashed with rain, you couldn't see Watford for water and South Mimms had just been declared a disaster area. There wasn't a human being in view for a 50-mile radius. "Perhaps they'll show up later," I said. He drove off slowly, looking for a fan to flee from.

Showbusiness golfers are strange people. They spend one half of their playing career at their club, moaning all the time about Japanese businessmen clogging up the course, and the other half at pro-celebrity events bellyaching that there is no-one on the course to interfere with their uninterrupted round.

I thought that next year we might make a virtue of the non-existent spectators and advertise my event as: "The Golf Tournament Where Even Lord Lucan Could Get Away With A Trouble-Free Round" or "Salman Rushdie Played In The Michael Parkinson Golf Classic And Nobody Noticed".

We could plant items in gossip columns whipping up public apathy, like "What happened to Shergar? The mystery was solved last night when the missing racehorse was won as first prize at the Michael Parkinson Golf Classic. The police said they were not interested".

I was able to contemplate such matters, and more, as I shouldered my way through the gale like a man breaking down a door. The wind was so strong that, at one hole, I drove the ball from the tee and then almost immediately shouted 'fore' to myself as the ball first held steady in the gale and then started in reverse.

It was shortly after that I met our other spectator. He turned out to be a photographer from the Yorkshire Golfer – a publication too new to be either choosey or blasé about who or what it takes pictures of. He said he wanted to take a shot of me in action.

In the end we settled for my executing a boring little chip-and-run. I talked him out of photographing my full swing on the grounds it might awaken public interest in the event.

Now I don't want you to run away with the idea that the tournament was a flop. On the contrary. We raised a few thousand quid for

Lord's Taverners. However, there is little doubt that, had the news of our joining the Exchange Rate Mechanism been more geared to the Michael Parkinson Golf Classic than the Tory Party Conference, then things might have been very different.

As it was, we concluded the day with an excellent dinner at which, in keeping with our modest profile, someone won a Monopoly set and another a book about the Yorkshire Dales.

What the day showed was that, if it be true that the definition of humour is the discrepancy between man's aspiration and man's achievement, the Michael Parkinson Golf Classic was a laugh from beginning to end.

I have never been one for early morning golf. Mid-morning tee-off is quite soon enough for me, mainly because my limbs don't start receiving messages from my brain until about 10 am. I made an exception at the weekend because one of my partners, Laurie Holloway, the piano player, had a gig later in the day and the third member of the team, the journalist and broadcaster Michael Barratt, simply likes playing early mainly I suspect because of the years he spent as a knocker-upper in his native Leeds.

Also it was Captain's Day, a chance to achieve golfing immortality by getting our names on the club-house wall. Most of all it was an opportunity to play the course when it had been pampered and cossetted for a special day. Unlike the rest of us, it looked a picture. Even under slate grey skies, the view from the high first tee across the valley to Bisham and Marlow justified the membership fees.

On a still day, the opening hole at Temple Golf Club is as hospitable as it is beautiful. However, when the wind whistles up the fairway and flattens your trouser legs against the horizon then it is not the hole at which you want to commence a medal round. Mr Holloway, who is the steadiest and best golfer of the three – a disciple of the Blue Danube backswing, da-dee-da-dum-dum – teed off at 6.50 for the first time, 6.55 for a second time and at 7 for the third and final time. There was, he thought, a touch of wind-induced Scarlatti in his swing. Whatever the reason, it did not augur well. The last time he lost two golf balls he was playing in Geraldo's band.

He took a nine on the first hole, I made a six. My drive would have gone further had it been hit by Lena Zavaroni, my seven iron from the rough nearly broke my wrists, my approach ended in a grass bunker to the right of the green whereupon I chipped to within three feet of the hole. I would have been satisfied with a bogey five. However my putt was of the palsied variety and I knew then that this was but the overture to a full-scale horror.

To be frank with you, I was not in the right frame of mind. I had prepared well. I had gone to bed early the night before with nothing more damaging than a cup of herbal tea. I had read *Power Driving, The Key To Distance and Accuracy*, pondered *The Art Of The Short Game* and devoured *Putting Made Simple*. My game-plan was to keep the driver in the bag until the back nine and concentrate on keeping the ball on the fairway. My thought for the day was: swing slow, finish high. I was programmed for success.

What sabotaged my plan was a question our secretary asked when we signed on at the clubhouse. He said to me: "I take it you will be entering the veterans' competition?" I suddenly realised I had qualified without being aware of my new status. The trick of growing older is to ignore the passing years. The problem is that other people won't let you. The last time I was confronted with the fact that I am no longer the lissom youth I see in my mind's eye was when an air hostess answered my complaint about bad service by patting me on the head and saying "There there old man. Keep your hair on."

What is particularly saddening about my arrival on the back nine of life, so to speak, is that, as far as golf is concerned, I didn't spend too much time on the front nine. It wasn't until my mid-40s that I relinquished my job as chairman and founder member of the Anti-Golf Society and started playing the game. I have gone very quickly from rabbit to veteran without acquiring a real history. It is as if I was born at the age of 45. Looking back to Saturday's game. I can see it was this confrontation with my own mortality prompted by our secretary's innocent question that upset my delicately balanced bio-rhythms.

If this sounds a trifle high falutin' then you ain't heard nothing yet. I believe that there is a mystical element in golf which often is the difference between a successful round and selling your clubs. Señor Ballesteros is the most eminent example of my theory. He has started winning again, looking again like the greatest golfer in the world.

Not too long ago some were writing him off. What has happened? Well the experts say he has changed his putter. They seek a practical solution and by doing so make my point. Is it a magic putter? Does it bear special qualities? Should we rush out and buy one and expect our game to improve?

Of course not. The fact is no-one, not even Seve, knows what is happening. You dare not ask in case it goes away, whatever it might be. It happens to all of us from time to time. We play a round of golf and suddenly it seems the easiest game in the world. The ball sings from the club, the chips roll to the pin, the putts drop. Other times you play like a dead donkey. Why? Who can tell? What we do know is that there never was a worried man who played a decent round of golf. Which is how I explain my awful performance on Captain's Day.

It is to my credit that it took a while for the wheels to come off. I struck the ball quite well but I couldn't putt. I tried the Crenshaw upright technique as well as the crouched style with the putter at 45 degrees to the green as favoured by Tommy Nakajima. None of it worked. I was thinking of trying Herr Langer's method. That's how golf can drive you crazy.

Looking back, the rot really set in on the seventh, a benign par four. Mr Barratt, who had been playing solidly, struck his second shot into the greenside bunker. There is nothing more risible in all sport than a golfer dressed and equipped like Nick Faldo trying to play a ball out of sand. Which is why golf is the ultimate test of sportsmanship and manners.

Bunkers have destroyed golfers, turned strong men into gibbering wrecks. They are the ultimate obstacles in life, the supreme test of character. I have played with men who have thrown all their clubs, followed by their bag and the trolley over cliffs after spending too long in a bunker. Sometimes they had to be restrained from following their equipment onto the rocks below. I have also played with men who faced with similar disasters, were so incredibly brave and humorous it made you proud to be marking their card. One chap I played with took six shots to get out of the bunker at Gleneagles and then putted back into the same bunker. All he said was "what a nuisance".

Therefore, when Mr Barratt stood in the bunker, sand-iron poised, he felt nothing but sympathy and best wishes flowing towards him from Mr Holloway and myself. He was sitting in the middle of the bunker on flat sand so we didn't anticipate too much drama. His first shot lifted the ball in the air, which is the general idea, but didn't move it forward so it plopped back to something like its original position. "Oh dear," said Mr Barratt. "Hard luck" we said. His second shot did exactly the same. "Damn," said Mr Barratt. We made reassuring sounds. His third shot moved the ball forward but not up in the air.

Mr Barratt was doing all the right things but not at the same time. "What is going on?" he asked. It was a rhetorical question. At the fourth attempt, he drove the ball into the face of the bunker, the crisis was increasing all the time, as were the comic possibilities.

"How many have I had in the bunker?" asked Mr Barratt. "Four" we told him. He looked so forlorn we wanted to adopt him. His next shot hit the underside lip of the bunker and flew behind him. "What am I doing wrong?" he asked. Mr Holloway suggested he take more sand. I managed to refrain from observing that there wasn't much left in the bunker, most of it having been deposited on the green which looked like Clacton beach.

Attempting to follow instructions and by now a desperate man, Mr Barratt took a lot of sand but no ball in his next attempt. As a consequence, the sand flew upwards and caught the prevailing wind, blew back in his face and covered his body. When the sandstorm died down he was so perfectly camouflaged we could barely see him.

It was at this point that I noticed Mr Holloway had a handkerchief in his mouth and his shoulders were shaking. My eyes were watering with suppressed mirth and I wanted to go to the toilet. The dam broke when the sand blasted figure in the bunker said "and what's so bloody funny". At least that's what we think he said. It came out as "Anwassoblurryunny" which is how a man speaks with a mouthful of sand.

The trouble with laughing uncontrollably is that from a distance it seems as if you might have been shot or are having a fit. The team coming up behind us told us later that they were gravely concerned to see two of us doubled up and holding our bellies as if being sick while the other member of the team – by this time Mr Barratt had seen the funny side of his predicament too – appeared to have collapsed in a writhing heap in the bunker.

In the end, Mr Barratt took seven shots to get out of the sand and scored an 11. Six holes later, on the short par three, he hit another bunker. "Here we go again," he said. When we got there, the ball had disappeared. We all saw it fall into the bunker but could find no trace of it. It was as if the bunker had opened up and swallowed the ball. We took it as a sign that the gods were not to be abused again. We played quietly to the clubhouse.

Mr Holloway had the best round and, in spite of his troubles, Mr Barratt played better than I did. Which gives you a fair idea of the kind of morning I had.

Later that day I watched Señor Ballesteros and the rest show us

how the game ought to be played. Of course they did have certain advantages.

For instance, no-one reminded Seve on the first tee that he wasn't getting any younger. On the other hand, if he took seven shots to get out of a bunker or played a round of golf like I did, then it would be a major disaster rather than a belly laugh.

The price you pay for perfection is the serious nature of the pursuit. Those of us who settle for less have much more fun.

Since my fateful round on Captain's Day I have played very little golf. I have not given up, or anything sensible like that. It is simply that I needed time to reassess my relationship with golf, to work out why it is I sometimes play with the rhythm and style of the young Gary Player and other times in the manner of an old and feeble prat.

What I am looking for is a level of mediocrity below which I never fall. The present situation is that there are no boundaries to my incompetence.

The trouble with writing about your misadventures is that they become enshrined in golfing folklore. For instance, the account of the round I played with Messrs Holloway and Barratt on Captain's Day at Temple Golf Club is to be hung in the clubhouse along with our scorecards.

There it will remain, to enable future generations to have a laugh at our incompetence. We have, I suppose, the consolation of immortality, but we would rather be living legends than dead ones.

What people will not understand when they read the article is that the three of us have had our moments, which we would willingly tell you about except no-one would be interested. Nowadays people are only interested in bad news, which is sad because I have played with Mr Barratt when he has looked like the best 20 handicapper in the world.

If he can avoid the bunkers and get his putter working he is a formidable opponent. His putter is an extraordinary implement, having a whirl of technicolor woods on its face. On the odd occasions he gets the head squared up with the hole he putts so sweetly that Messrs Rice and Lloyd-Webber should consider re-uniting to write the musical about it . . . "Barratt and The Amazing Technicolor Dreamputter".

Similarly, I have played with Mr Holloway when his swing was so graceful and fluent it looked like Johnny Hodges sounds. I told him this once, but he said he would rather be compared with Ben

Webster. He can be a touch pedantic about music.

None the less, there was a time some years ago when, as a humble 17 handicapper, he broke the course record by shooting a gross 76, nett 59. No-one wrote an article about that. Nor was it recorded, until now, that two years ago I stood with Mr Holloway on the 18th at Temple needing to sink a tiddly putt to beat his record by one shot. I lipped out and equalled Mr Holloway's performance.

I became a 12-handicap golfer, like Mr Holloway, and things have gone downhill ever since. Even so, I did have that moment of glory when golf seemed the easiest game in the world and I was convinced that if I kept at it I would soon be earning a fortune with Gary, Lee and Chi-Chi on the Seniors' Tour.

I was talking about this very subject the other day with Mr Holloway. He had called round to ask if I kept my card for Captain's Day because they were going to frame it. I had, of course, torn it up on the 11th, where, with all shots gone, I placed my approach to the green nearer Bisham Abbey than the flag. Nonetheless, I had no problem reliving the horror: I started with a six on a par four and then went 6 (4), 5 (4), 6 (5), 4 (3), 6 (4), 3 (4), 4 (3), 6 (5), 5 (3) and finished on the 11th with a five-wood towards Marlow via Bisham.

I completed a new card, signed it and handed it to Mr Holloway. As he scrutinised it I said: "Do you remember when I equalled your score at Temple?" He said: "Yes I do." Then he said, almost to himself: "He must have been possessed." I hope they don't make too much fuss about hanging the article and the scorecards. It could have a grievous effect upon my rehabilitation.

Generally speaking people have been very kind. Apart from letters of commiseration, I have received three videos featuring advice by Tom Kite, Seve Ballesteros and Nick Faldo and an anonymous donor sent me a book called *The Inner Game Of Golf*. I was also sent a pamphlet listing alternative hobbies for senior citizens such as doing tapestry and making tea cosies. I suspect this came from my friend Mr Tarbuck.

To be frank, I have discovered that the only consolation for a bad round of golf is to find someone who is worse off than you are. It is why, on these occasions, I look towards my pal Al. His theory about golf is that it was invented as certain proof that life was not meant to be easy. He believes that the selling of golf as a leisure pursuit is a fraud and that golf bags, particularly those sold to middle-aged golfers, should carry a health warning.

He eschews golf lessons and coaching manuals and puts his faith in technology. At one time or another he has had the entire history of golf engineering in his bag, often all at the same time. He has the biggest and heaviest golf bag I have ever seen. Caddies scatter and feign injury as he approaches the pro's shop. Of those who dare to carry for him only the few trained by the Long Range Desert Group to survive like camels come through the ordeal unscathed.

He took up golf because his doctor suggested it might be a good way to relieve the tensions and frustrations of his job. He now looks forward to work as a relief from golf and the doctor gives him tranquillisers to get him on the course. He is sometimes known as "Two Gloves Al" because he wears a glove on either hand.

This stops him biting his nails down to the second knuckle during a round. Although he refuses to pay for expert advice he is willing to listen to anyone with a theory about how to play the game. The other day he met a man in a pub who told him that the perfect posture at address was to imagine he was sitting on a bar stool.

At the same time another customer suggested that he might find it easier hitting the ball if he widened his stance. You don't have to be clever to understand that the two pieces of advice are incompatible. None the less, my pal Al has managed to incorporate them both in his set-up. So if you see a man squatting on a golf course looking like a bandy-legged fellow trying to sit on a tall bar stool, you will have met my pal.

In his unremitting search for sorrow and aggravation on the golf course he has travelled where few have been. The tranquillisers he uses are the kind given to animals to make their trip to the slaughterhouse seem a pleasant one and they give his temper in moments of stress a benign malevolence.

Once, after he had seven-putted on a par-three after finishing 5ft from the pin with his tee shot, he inquired of his caddie: "Do you know what I would do if the man who invented golf walked on to this green right now?" The caddie shook his head. "I would poke his eyes out with my putter," said Al, affably enough.

He is much concerned with metaphysical and philosophical issues raised by the game, such as: If golf is a metaphor for man's struggle against his environment why was it necessary to invent bunkers? Another of his concerns is how the man who invents a missile capable of entering a building through a keyhole from 100 miles away can be the same fellow who misses a 2ft putt.

I have yet to discuss with him the latest theory on the subject of putting. This comes from a sports psychologist who suggests that random recitation can cure the yips. Dr Richard Masters, of York University, says that we should forget teaching manuals and start reciting letters of the alphabet when putting, especially for money. What Al will make of this I do not know.

His current thinking on the subject is that the lining up of the putt is best done from a horizontal position. What he does is flatten himself on the green and sight his putter head behind the ball. The difficult part is getting to his feet while keeping the putter in the correct position. He thinks the solution might be a putter he can use from a kneeling position. What the R & A will make of all this is anybody's guess.

The other day I met one of my great heroes, Mr Gary Player, who kindly asked me about my game. When I told him, he suggested the only way out of my predicament was practice. It was sensible and kindly advice, but not what I wanted to hear. For all I admire Mr Player, my pal Al remains my role model.

The fact is we enjoy our pursuit of mediocrity and I suspect that, in the unlikely event of us becoming as good as Mr Player, we would give the game up and find something else to bellyache about.

As you know I have always been sceptical of the so-called pressures of modern sport. I think pressure is being unemployed or homeless, not about getting up in the morning and having no greater worry than playing a round of golf for a living or kicking a football for 10 grand a week.

Having said all that, I must admit that when Herr Langer stood over that putt on the 18th to settle the Ryder Cup, I was hiding behind our settee with my hands over my eyes. The wife had to go for a lie-down and she's not been the same woman since. It has affected her golf (more of that later). I think she's in mourning.

What the last act of the drama at Kiawah Island demonstrated to all of us, particularly the players, was that pressure is not, as is commonly supposed, about missing a putt if you've already been paid $50,000 just to turn up, and know that, in any case, there's a couple of million in the bank.

What it showed is it really matters when you are putting to decide the fate of your team and their supporters.

I had a similar moment playing at Collingtree Park near Northampton. This is a new and splendid course which we played in a fourball competition for the Variety Club. I must say I played the front nine to my great satisfaction, scoring 23 Stableford points. Our team total was 46 and as we came to the turn we were in the lead and good heart.

Our trouble started on the 11th when, with two of our team losing balls in the lake, our fourball reached the green with a combined total of 22 shots. When I tell you I was in a greenside bunker for two, you will understand what a terrible struggle my team-mates had to get the ball somewhere near the flag. I was the hope of my side. If I could get up and down in two we would have three points and at least maintain our momentum.

I opened my stance just like José Maria and imagined the commentary by Peter: "This is where he reaps the dividend of all those lonely hours of practice . . ." I took what I imagined to be a long slow swing, aiming two inches behind the ball and sent it hurtling out of the bunker, one bounce into the bunker opposite.

Never mind. Get it out, sink the putt and we still have two points. Forget José Maria. He never could play anyway. This time you are Nick and you want a high stopper. The ball is sitting up in the bunker and there's about 20ft to the pin. Close the face a bit, break the wrists quickly, get it up and out. Just like the video. In the video the ball lobs out of the bunker and stops six inches from the flag. In real life it rose vertically from the depths like a dolphin at feeding time and plonked deep into the front fringe of the bunker.

Think positively. Chip it out and in and we still have one point.

My problem was that there is no coaching manual I know of, no video I have seen, which shows you how to play a chip with one foot in a deep bunker and the other leg atop. At a rough guess the shot would be best attempted by a man with one leg four feet longer than the other. As it was, I attempted to play the ball by standing in the bunker with my back to the hole, trying to hit the ball with what can only be described as a paddling shot. I looked like a man escaping down river in a canoe.

It says much for the strength and resilience of my team that our challenge did not crumple at this point. In fact, we rallied and as we came to the last hole, we were in a situation where six points would make the difference between winning a bronze figurine of a man lining up a putt, or an umbrella.

Now the 18th at Collingtree is worthy of careful explanation because it is one of the most demanding finishing holes your correspondent has come across.

It is a par-five requiring a cautious drive alongside a lake and a carefully judged second shot into an area bounded by bunkers and water to face the challenge of a moated green. With a drive, a six-iron and a seven-iron I was on the green in regulation and thinking of turning pro. I was 20ft from the flag. From a distance it looked a certain five.

It was not until I reached the green that I realised the designer had decided to have the last laugh. He had sloped the green left to right towards the water and filled it with secret gullies and hidden undulations.

I looked at the putt for a long time and didn't have an idea where the ball was going. I took four putts to get down and even now I couldn't tell you how I got the ball in the hole.

My only consolation is the certain knowledge that better players than I will do the same, and worse, in the future. That is the joy of golf: the understanding that no matter how badly you play there is someone, somewhere, having an even more desperate time. That very evening, watching the telly from behind the furniture, I knew for a certain fact that Bernhard Langer would have swapped his five at Kiawah Island for my seven at Collingtree Park.

I don't know how Bernhard went about his rehabilitation, but I settled for a round of golf with the wife at Wentworth. We played the new Edinburgh course, which is as tough to play as it is beautiful to behold.

The first hole gives a fair indication of what you are in for. From a raised tee you have a fair chance of seeing the flag on the green if you are blessed with perfect eyesight, the weather is crystal clear and you are using a Field Marshal's binoculars. It leads you into hitherto unexplored areas of Wentworth estate, some so remote and private they are worthy of a visit by David Attenborough.

The virtue of playing with the wife is that you can have a row without ruining a beautiful friendship. The fact is we were both a bit testy because of losing the Ryder Cup to the Yanks and also having been behind a Japanese fourball at Gleneagles the week before. Both experiences had taken a lot out of us.

What I cannot understand is the discrepancy between the acknowledged efficiency of the Japanese in business matters and their inability to play a round of golf in less time that it takes to make several hundred motor cars. This question needs urgently addressing if we are not to reach a situation where golf on British courses will have to be conducted under supervision of a United Nations peacekeeping force.

All this is by way of explaining that we were not in the best of moods to tackle the problems set by a course as testing as the Edinburgh. We decided to walk off at the 13th. Because the course is new we had little idea of where we were in relation to the clubhouse. I set off in the lead, partly because I wasn't talking to the wife but mainly because I am the acknowledged pathfinder in the family.

We reached a crossroads. "Left," I said. "Straight ahead," said the wife. This is a woman who has to be given a road map to get to the local shops. I ignored her and forked left. She followed, muttering. We had been walking for 20 minutes when I began to think something was wrong. We came to another crossroads. "Straight on," I said. "Right," said the wife, her voice becoming enfeebled by fatigue. I saw a clearing ahead and heard the sound of traffic. We headed towards it like thirsty souls seeing an oasis. Which is how we came to be standing on the A30 somewhere between the Chertsey turn-off and Chiquito's Mexican restaurant fully dressed for a round of golf and pulling large bags on trolleys.

We were not, it must be said, the kind of people you normally find hitch-hiking on a dual carriageway. Several cars slowed down to have a look at us as if we were Martians newly landed. One young man recognised me and shouted: "I didn't know you could hit 'em this far, Parky". I waved in nonchalant manner pretending I was going to a fancy dress party, while the wife muttered something behind me which sounded like "You prat".

We made it back to the clubhouse about an hour later. Bernard Gallacher, lately arrived back from Kiawah Island, was outside the pro's shop. He too had suffered a hard day.

"You are not going to tell me you could have sunk the putt that Bernhard missed?" he said. I shook my head. It wasn't that I didn't have an opinion. I was simply too knackered to speak.

What I wanted to say was that no matter how long they play, the pros will never know the real problems faced everyday by thousands of ordinary golfers.

Like I've always said: they don't know what real pressure is.

"The magic's gone," said the wife. "If this is the parting of the ways can I have custody of the Wisdens?" I said.

"I'm not talking about our marriage you twerp. The magic has gone from my golf," she said.

I said I was relieved, although it didn't take me long to work out that a divorce would be considerably cheaper than my wife's continued search for perfection on the golf course. She has propped up the economy of several countries by her generous and dedicated support of local golf professionals and throughout the world there are teachers and caddies whose eyes light up when they hear Mrs Parkinson is on the way to pay a visit.

If she asked me what's wrong – which she never does – I would have to tell her that I think she is confused. She has been taught so many different techniques that her mind is in a turmoil at address.

She will try anything. In Australia I found her on a practice range with her upper arms pinioned by a webbing strap and a soccer ball between her knees.

I should say that the pro was similarly constrained and both were practising a method devised by Mr Leadbetter in America. Or so they said.

Whatever they were doing, it didn't look like a lot of fun, so I didn't pursue the matter further.

There was, however, one occasion when I thought things had gone too far. The problem is that my wife is a warm and friendly soul who has never yet met a golf pro she didn't want to adopt. She was particularly pleased by a pro in Spain whom, she felt, understood her game and made her play better.

One day when I went to pick her up from her lesson I saw the pro lifting his shirt and the wife staring intently at what was on view.

"What on earth is going on?" I asked, sounding like the affronted husband. "Juan is showing me his operation scars," she said.

It is sad when someone who has such dedication and love for golf becomes depressed by it. So when the wife announced that the magic had departed her game I broke the rule of a lifetime and said I would play a round of winter golf. My attitude to winter golf is cautious. I see no sense in dressing up like a lighthouse keeper to play a round of golf. Normally I am seen on a course between December and March only in exceptional circumstances.

I came to this decision after playing Gleneagles on a wincingly cold day. I remember because I was wearing ladies' tights for the first time. They are far and away the most efficient and comfortable means of keeping your legs warm but putting them on in the locker room is not advised in areas unaccustomed to the modern trend of what is known in some quarters as bi-fashion and others as cross-dressing.

The other problem with wearing tights is how the wearer would face the crisis of being taken ill on the course and having to explain to the ambulance man how he came to be wearing a pair of ladies' 15-denier pantyhose.

I do not know what my partner at Gleneagles was wearing under his trousers but he had on his head the most remarkable hat I have ever seen. Constructed of wool and waterproof plastic it had a neck flap to stop the water running down his neck. There was a large peak at the front to keep the water from his eyes and ear flaps which he strapped to the side of his face by tying the end under his chin. He looked like a survivor of the retreat from Leningrad.

When we reached the highest part of the course he stood on the tee and looked around him. His eyes were running, two candles fell from his nose, there was frost on his eyebrows and his lips were cracked and chapped.

And do you know what he said to me? "It's a beautiful game, golf, isn't it". And he meant it.

Since then I have been careful about playing golf in the winter, but clearly the crisis in the wife's life took precedence over my ambition never to be cold on a golf course again.

So off we went to regain the magic. I teed off, walked over to my wife on the ladies' tee and together we strolled down the first. I found my ball and was surprised I couldn't see the wife's ball on the fairway, since the last time she missed the cut stuff, Jim Callaghan was the Prime Minister. We searched for her ball, she moaning the while that this was certain proof the magic had gone forever and me nearly believing her.

We were joined by two greenkeepers and then by a friendly four-ball making their way back to the clubhouse. There were now eight of us engaged in trying to find the wife's ball. We must have looked like a line of volunteers helping the police in an inch-by-inch search for clues.

Finally I said to her: "Think back to the tee. What sort of shot did you play? Did you hit it well?"

The search stopped as she pondered the question. Our future strategy depended upon her reply.

"Oh, my God," she said. "What is it?" I cried. "I didn't hit the ball at all," she said.

"You missed it?" I said.

"No. I forgot to take the drive," she said.

Later, in the clubhouse, the general consensus was that they had never heard anything like it. We could all tell stories of drives that ended up in trees, or down a rabbit hole or in the back of a passing lorry. I once drove the ball in the opposite direction to the fairway, having been given the line by a partner with a suspect sense of humour. But none of us could recall an instance where the player forgot to take a shot.

It has to be reported that the wife made light of her forgetfulness. By the time we reached the 16th I was three down with three to play, which is the way it has always been and no doubt ever will be. She won the game on the 18th by chipping in for a birdie.

"Magic," I said. She gave me an old-fashioned look.

Providing she remembers in future to take every shot, I can see little wrong with her game. Mind you, I'm the last person you should ask about magic. If you've never had it, how do you know what you are looking for?

Portugal was stirring from hibernation. The sun shone every day, gently thawing out winter bones, and when the cloud came it was as flimsy as a bride's veil.

It was perfect weather for The Jimmy Tarbuck Golf Classic, which this year took place on the San Lorenzo course in the Algarve and in several karaoke bars.

At the end of the week it was demonstrable that those who had spent most time practising karaoke did not return the best scores. On the other hand, they looked like they had had a good time, which is more than can be said for one or two of the prizewinners who appeared to require the services of a counsellor in post-competition stress.

The fact is that while most of us might entertain thoughts of emulating our heroes and playing golf for a living, few of us realise how tiring it is pretending to be a professional golfer. The strain showed on our foursome fairly early in the week when High Handicapper asked our captain what he should do.

Without inspecting the predicament our captain said through clenched teeth: "Hit the ball as hard as you can, as far as you can – and as quickly as you can."

Not being a sensitive fellow, High Handicapper took our captain at his word and almost swung himself off his feet in an effort to follow instructions. The outcome was the most dreadful slice into a pine forest. We trooped in search, moving slowly like mourners, faces set grim.

Looking at us you would not have imagined we were on holiday and having a lovely time. When we found the ball it was behind a tree, lying against a root, as safe from human hand as a fox in its lair.

We looked at the disaster. High Handicapper said: "What shall I do?" Only a vein throbbing in our captain's forehead showed how fiercely he fought to retain self-control.

Looking his team-mate in the eye, he said: "Well it seems to me you have two options. One is you can find a phone box, look through yellow pages and find a lumberjack. Then you could call him and ask him to come down here with his equipment and chop down yonder pine.

"If, in the meantime, he could also dig up the root without moving your ball you might conceivably be able to chip out on to the fairway. Failing that you could pick up and leave the scoring on this hole to the rest of us in which case we might get back to the clubhouse before the holiday is over."

High Handicapper considered these options for a moment and then said: "I think I'd better pick up."

Golf gives wonderful insights into the human psyche. By narrowing our ambitions to the seemingly simple proposition of getting a ball into a small hole in the ground it reveals the basic man. Our High Handicapper is a discernible type familiar to anyone who has ever played a round of golf.

He always asks the most obvious questions. My theory is that when he asks: "What shall I do?" when the answer is plain, he is merely transferring responsibility to his playing partner.

If he messes up your instructions he gives you a dirty look and tells them in the clubhouse you cost him the hole. If the shot comes off he will walk away in triumph as if it was always his own idea.

These players are also the ones who have a complete lexicon of drivel to accompany every bad shot. They hook the ball off the tee and, as it screams towards the tree-line, shout "Catch the wind" or "Fade" as if there was a master plan attached to their incompetence.

My favourite is the badly aimed shot going 70 yards wide of the target accompanied by this commentary from the striker: "Turn . . . why doesn't it turn? Just look at it going straight on. Keep left. Where's the wind? Come on wind. Bend on the wind, ball. Come left." Inevitably the ball ignores these instructions and disappears into the undergrowth whereupon the golfer turns to his companions and says: "Would you believe it?"

These are the players who never get a good lie on the fairway, who are always in bunkers that have been robbed of sand and who have never had a putt which wasn't sabotaged by a sprig mark or a hidden borrow. If golf is a test of character it is not because of the game itself but the company we keep.

Needless to say our team did not feature among the prizewinners.

Our triumph was that we finished still speaking to one another. The real bonus of the trip was the discovery of a wonderful golf course. San Lorenzo is not the longest golf course in Europe but it's one of the toughest.

It has a beguiling start, par five, par three and two par fours, one dog-leg left, the other dog-leg right. Nothing too tough and you feel quite pleased with yourself as you reach the high ground and come in view of the Atlantic.

What faces you is one of those awkward par threes, 130 yards across a chasm to the green, stroke index 17. It is when you move to the next tee that the real test begins.

From the sixth tee you can see a lot of the Atlantic Ocean and not much of the fairway which follows the contours of the coastline turning left towards the green. The prevailing wind is off the sea and into your face.

The next hole similarly hugs the coastline while the eighth is one of the most difficult par fives you will ever play. To start with it is 570 yards long. It turns inland but towards more water in the form of a large lake. The green itself is reached across water and the landing area looks as narrow as a surfboard.

The back nine is even more spectacular than the front with pine trees and flowering almond blossom and views of distant hills the colour and shape of sleeping elephants.

The finishing hole is one of the most spectacular I have ever played. The drive skirts a lake, the second shot is across another lake to a green surrounded by bunkers. On the other hand, if you are either very brave or extremely foolhardy you could try to drive across the lake towards the green from the tee. You had better be able to hit the driver in excess of 270 yards otherwise you are in trouble.

I have described the course because it is worth remarking on, but also to give you the setting for one of the most remarkable comebacks ever seen in modern golf. I am talking about the match between myself and my partner, Irish Joe the Pro, and the two lads who own the karaoke club, John and Jeremy.

They were big lads and gave the ball a terrible spank. Joe is not short off the tee either, in fact he's a long hitter for a man about to collect his bus pass. His real talent is that he's an Irish golfer, which is to say a conjurer of shots, as adept with the back of a club as the face of it.

We started quite well by halving the first hole. However, when we came to the sixth with the sun sparkling off the Atlantic and the sea birds wheeling, we were four down. "What do we do partner?" I asked Joe. "Nivver fear. This is where the course begins and where superior tactics will decide the match," said my partner.

At that precise moment, Jeremy hit a drive which started off towards America, swung left along the edge of the sea and landed on the centre of the fairway a nine-iron from the green. Which is how it came to pass that with six holes played we were five down.

"Things are desperate," I said to my partner. Whereupon he came out with one of the great lines in modern sport. "Just let's keep playing the way we are," he said. Only an Irishman could say such a thing and mean it. I said: "Joe, if we keep on playing the way we are, we will be finished after the 11th hole."

His optimism reminded me of Matt Busby's memorable advice to his team in the semi-final of the European Cup in Madrid when they were two down at half-time and, to all intents and purposes, finished. He put his head round the dressing room door, contemplated the scene of abject misery and said: "All right lads. Just keep on playing fitba."

It was also reminiscent in its sanguine approach to impending disaster to the moment when Graham Stevenson, the Yorkshire cricketer, walked to the wicket for England at Sydney last man in with 20 needed to win.

There were 50,000 Australians baying for blood around the ground and in the middle a welcoming committee of more Australians who wasted little time in informing Stevenson that he was an unwelcome Pom and illegitimate to boot.

He was greeted by his fellow Yorkshireman David Bairstow, who said to him, by way of an invitation to a tactical discussion: "What tha' reckon then Stevo?" Whereupon his friend surveyed the scene, the lights, the noise, the insults and the scoreboard showing they needed to score 20 to win the match for their country and said: "It's nice out here, innit?"

It must be said that my partner didn't exactly follow his own advice. He started playing much better so that we reached the 10th only three down.

The turning point on the back nine came when our opponents drove into the pines and instead of playing out elected to go for the

green through the kind of forest thick enough to hide a squadron of tanks. They more or less hit out simultaneously, one shot sounding like the echo of the other.

Standing on the fairway with Joe I witnessed the most extraordinary sight. As the balls ricocheted around the pines, trimming branches and lopping tops, so the natural inhabitants of the wood took flight. The air was thick with fleeing birds, furry animals broke cover and ran for their lives across the fairway.

It looked like the scene from *Bambi* when the hunters comb the woods. "I've nivver seen anythin' like that," said the Irishman preparing to win the hole unhindered by opponents.

As we walked off the green, there were carrion birds circling the forest inspecting the debris for casualties. We won the next two holes and halved the match.

Funny game golf . . . and unpredictable too – thank the Lord.

Our cricket season started under winter skies with arctic winds. It would not have been a surprise to have come across a polar bear in the car park or witnessed the heavy roller being pulled by a team of huskies.

Given the conditions the perfect team would have been: Captain Scott, Franz Klammer, David Vine, Eskimo Nell, Magnus Magnusson, Sonja Henie, Jean Claude Killy, Nanook of the North, Roald Amundsen and Torvill and Dean. Twelfth man: Captain Oates.

As a joke, one of our batsmen stopped the bowler from the river end in his delivery stride and complained to the umpire of an iceberg moving behind the bowler's arm. Our umpire can normally see the funny side of things but on this occasion was not amused, having lost the will to live despite the fact that he was wearing three pairs of interlocking combinations, a balaclava, a scarf and a polo neck sweater.

One of the few consolations of growing older is that you can spend such days in the warmth of the bar rather than having to brave it out in the middle. I used to hate the start of the new season. It always seemed to take us to Bramall Lane against Sheffield or Headingley to play Leeds. Neither were idyllic, even in mid-summer with the roses blooming. On an early spring day in Yorkshire, with your fingers like icicles and the face leaking from every orifice, they were severe tests of character and determination.

In the days when I played for Barnsley, Mr George Henry Pope used to preside over Bramall Lane. He was professional and groundsman and under both guises delighted in demonstrating to young cricketers who thought they knew a thing or two the intricate art of swing and seam bowling.

He left little to chance. As groundsman, he made sure there was enough grass on the wicket to take the seam; as a professional of great and deserved reputation he felt free to give his comments and predictions on events. Thus, within earshot of the dressing room, he would

opine that the opposition would be lucky to make 50 and he would most certainly be on a collection.

I suppose I was 16 or 17 when I first played against Sheffield and Mr Pope. It was the first game of the season. It was gloomy and cold with fat, dark clouds sitting on top of the soccer stand.

It wasn't the loveliest ground in the world, but it might have been the most intimidating. In those days the cricket club shared the ground with Sheffield United Football Club and behind Mr Pope, as he ran in to bowl, was the dark and mysterious emptiness of the soccer stand. What it told you as you scanned the terraces from the middle was that this was a ground where serious business took place. If you came here to enjoy yourself, forget it.

In those days I opened with Dickie Bird and the only consolation was that if you thought I was nervous, then you should have seen my partner. Mr Bird was a fine player but possessed of the nervous disposition of a squirrel. He is the only man I know who used to bite his finger-nails through his batting gloves. He would turn up for the start of a season with a brand new pair of gloves and after three games he wouldn't have a finger-top left on them.

His other peculiarity was a desire to give all his gear away if ever he had a bad trot. He was cured of this when he did it once too often and his team-mates – who had hitherto always returned his gear when asked – made him buy it back.

I am certain Mr Bird was my partner that day at Bramall Lane when we walked out to take part in Mr Pope's master class. I remember we were bowled out for under 50, that Mr Pope took eight wickets and that he made the ball do everything except sit up and sing "The Rose of Tralee."

I faced him for about eight overs and I don't recall ever getting the bat near the ball. He swung it both ways, seamed it and cut it about. He made it hum through the air and dance from the wicket.

All of it was accompanied by his relentless, non-stop commentary, thus: "Oh a little leg cutter there I think. Went a bit did that. Possibly too much," Or: "Nice outswinger, George. Too good for the opposition perhaps."

His most intimate asides were directed at the umpire. The relationship had already been established before a ball had been bowled. As George handed his sweater to the official he would say: "Good afternoon Mr Umpire. How nice to see you again. And how are the prize

marrows this year?" The umpire would be flattered that the great man had remembered his vegetables and would beam benignly.

"And the wife and two daughters?" George would inquire. By this time the relationship was such that the umpire was certain that George Henry Pope was a long lost relative. George was much too subtle to take immediate advantage. The first time he hit your pads he would give a long look, stifle an appeal and say to the umpire: "A little too high perhaps."

But the next time it would be "Owzat" at full volume with the umpire eager to oblige. I played against him three times and once I hit him for a boundary. I played him through mid-wicket for four. That was nearly 40 years ago and I was so proud I can still remember what it sounded like as it came off the bat. I also recall that next ball he knocked my off peg out of the ground.

The first time I opened the season at Headingley against Leeds is also engraved deep on my memory, not to say etched on my soul. I never liked Headingley. I still don't. It lacks character and feels like it doesn't belong. It doesn't belong to the Yorkshire County Cricket Club, which is probably part of the trouble. But I think the real problem was that whenever I played there it always seemed to be 250 for one with Leeds batting and Dickie Bird and I worrying about padding up and going out to face the likes of the young Fred Trueman.

The first time I played at Headingley there was one spectator and he sat in lonely splendour while Billy Sutcliffe and the Australian rugby league international Arthur Clues smashed a century apiece against us.

I didn't count but it seemed to me as if about 170 of their 200 runs went past me at cover point. A good many ended at the feet of the solitary spectator, who would watch me in critical silence as I ran the fifty yards to retrieve the ball.

I decided to appeal to his better nature, saying: "You might throw the ball back to save me running down here all the time." He looked at me quizzically. "Nay lad," he said. "Tha' misunderstands. I've come here to watch *thee* work not to do any missen."

What cricketers realise is that no matter how horrendous the first game of the season might be in terms of weather and lack of form, it is nothing compared to the awful pain that tortures the body next morning. The stretching and exercising of joints and muscles which have been dormant throughout the winter promotes an awful pain and stiffness.

I do not exaggerate when I say that on more than one occasion I have been rolled from my bed the morning after the first game. I found that if the wife could propel me from the marital couch I would make it on my hands and knees to the bathroom where, by using the towel rail and the edge of the wash basin, I could raise myself to a standing position. I could shave only by lowering my head to my hand because I couldn't raise my arm to my chin.

Going to work was a problem. For a day or two after the first game I could only walk if I did my famous imitation of Groucho Marx, I remember one occasion – when I had also suffered a smack on the bridge of the nose during the first game, which left me with two splendid black eyes – that when I grouchoed onto the train the next morning, a middle-aged woman gave me a piteous look and offered her seat. What is more, I took it.

Nowadays I don't have those problems. I don't make an appearance on the greensward until June is nearly out and only then if the sun is melting the big roller. When on the field I turn my arm over from a standing position and field at first slip, standing so close to the wicket-keeper that often I am to be found behind him. As a batsman I am delighted if I can hit far enough to call "wait" to my partner. I am, to quote J J Warr (and one must never tire of quoting the classics), in the springtime of my sporting senility.

What you never lose is the keen anticipation of the new season. On Saturday I walked round our ground and by the time I had travelled from one sightscreen to the other it had gone from bright but chilly sunshine to sleet being driven on a wind with the cutting edge of a chainsaw. The outfield has sand on it where the hockey players have been, the seats need a lick of paint, the hedges are bare of leaf. Swept by sleet and rain, the ground had a desolate look.

Any outsider witnessing the scene would think it an unseemly introduction to a game of such elegant reputation. What those of us who know realise is that there will soon be days of unending summer when we shall see white warriors on green meadows. There will also be days when the drone of summer, the smell of cut grass, and the sound of cricket will produce a cocktail so potent that a sip could be fatal. What happens is you pass out in a deckchair. And when you wake up you think you've died and gone to heaven.

The marvellous thing about cricket is that you can have a better time when it rains than when it shines. In other words, often the conversation is an improvement on the cricket.

Visiting the Long Room bar the other day I came across Alan Revill, of Derbyshire and Leicestershire, and Keith Andrew of Northants and England. Mr Revill is one of those people who lives his life according to the cricket season. It is not known what he does during the football season, although it has been rumoured that he hibernates. When asked how long he has been married he will say he "opened the innings in 1953".

In a restaurant he will ask the waitress for "the batting order" (the menu) and the "score card" (the bill). We once spent a glorious summer day together, drinking good wine and telling tales. When the time came to go he surveyed my garden, cocked an ear to the birds, raised his face to the sun and said: "I think we'll bat Parky old lad."

At Lord's we talked of life's mysteries, like how George Henry Pope bowled his leg-cutter and why Leslie Jackson, who took more than 1,700 first-class wickets at a cost of little over 17 apiece, only played twice for England. This led us to ask the same of Mr Andrew who, although by common consent was the finest wicket-keeper of his generation, also only played twice for his country.

Keith's first Test was against Australia at Brisbane in the 54–55 series when England lost by an innings and 154 runs and went on to win the next four games in what became known as Tyson's series. Keith said that Tyson was at his quickest when something or someone upset him. When this happened, Keith said, it was advisable to move back five yards or so.

I once asked Keith Miller how quick Tyson was. Keith said he couldn't tell because he never managed to see a ball he bowled him. I also asked Dennis Lillee what was the quickest he had ever bowled; he said the fastest ball he ever delivered was during a league game when he was playing in Lancashire.

The unfortunate batsman was struck on the leg by Lillee's missile, whereupon the Australian appealed. The umpire gave the batsman out but, much to Lillee's annoyance, he didn't move. "You're out," Dennis said (or words to that effect).

The batsman looked at the bowler through pain filled eyes and said: 'I'd love to go Dennis but I daren't move. I think you've broken my bloody leg." And he wasn't fibbing or imagining things.

"Time to put the covers on," said Mr Revill, by way of announcing that we would need an umbrella to get to the car park. We splashed

by the Grace Gates. Looking back through the rain Lord's looked like a moated castle. The next day they abandoned play. This was the sign we had all been waiting for; confirmation at last that the cricket season had begun.

When I was born my father, certain he had produced an opening bat for Yorkshire and England, set about finding a suitable cricketer's name. His first suggestion was that I be called Herbert Hedley Parkinson in honour of Sutcliffe and Verity, my father's heroes. When this was vetoed by my mother he suggested Michael Melbourne Parkinson in celebration of a recent victory by England in that city.

It would have been worse had we won in Adelaide.

Fortunately my mother, a woman of great commonsense, would have none of it and plain Michael it was. My mother had not realised when she married my father that she was taking on the Yorkshire County Cricket Club as well.

The realisation first dawned on her honeymoon, which father persuaded her to take in London. The trip from Barnsley to London in those days was a glamorous one and my mother was overjoyed at his thoughtfulness.

What she didn't realise was that Yorkshire were playing Middlesex at Lord's and she spent three days behind the bowler's arm while her husband sat, as he always did at any cricket match, with a huge smile on his face as if he was the happiest man on the planet.

By the time I had arrived upon Yorkshire soil and was able to stand up and hold a cricket bat, my mother had become a fair all-rounder. She averaged over 20 on Scarborough beach and was a useful donkey-drop bowler. Her sister, Auntie Madge, was our wicket-keeper and there have been few better standing up using a coat. They were both coached by my father, who believed anyone born in Yorkshire, man or woman, had a duty to play cricket.

Indeed, as I grew up and started playing street cricket I often picked Eunice Bradbury in my side. She was as pretty as a picture and slender as a cane, but she could throw a cricket ball through a brick wall.

We played cricket all the time. When I look back at my youth it was one long cricket match interrupted now and then by totally

unnecessary matters like learning algebra or conjugating Latin verbs.

The first floodlit cricket match did not take place in Australia. It took place in the mining village of Cudworth outside No 10 Moorland Terrace where our street lamp became the wicket and we played under flickering gas light until they called us in.

When it was really dark you couldn't see the bowler as he ran up. This disadvantage to the batsman was evened out by the fact that the bowler's run-up meant he had one leg in the gutter and the other on the pavement.

This accounted for the appearance in local cricket of certain bowlers whose run to the wicket gave every indication that they were wearing a surgical boot. I once batted for four nights scoring 1,027 not out, a record not likely to be beaten in my lifetime. Although my mate Barrie came near it, once scoring 1,010 before being run out in dubious circumstances when he left his crease to go to the toilet.

There was not a single person in our street games, not a boy or a girl, who didn't have the ambition to play for Yorkshire. It wasn't so much you wanted to as it was expected of you. As soon as you were big enough you played League cricket. In those days there were no friendly fixtures in Yorkshire. The Leagues were the spawning grounds of Yorkshire cricket. They were trawled with a fine mesh and the county missed very little. My apprenticeship in this cricket came when I was 11-years-old and played in a team captained by my father. I learned a lot from him, particularly about the art of psychological warfare.

He was an expert at allusion, creating uncertainty among his opponents. I remember one day when he introduced a new fast bowler the opposition had never seen before. After the first over their opening bat said to my father: "By gum, John Willie, but your new lad's a bit quick." And my father said: "He is that. But tha' should have seen him before he got gassed."

It was tough cricket, as far removed from the romantic image as could be imagined. Where there should have been blue hills in the distance we had muckstacks, instead of deckchairs there were hard wooden benches and the men who sat on them had not come to enjoy themselves. Their job in life was to make the players miserable, to give them some stick. We travelled to away games in a coal lorry and often arrived looking like a touring version of the Black and White Minstrels.

Youngsters, no matter how tender, were given no quarter. It was assumed if you were picked to play in the League you could look after yourself. If you couldn't then tough. I remember my father being worked over by a young fast bowler who, after hitting him several times, finally offered a smirky, fairly sarcastic "Sorry". Whereupon my old man said: "Nay, don't apologise lad, it's my turn next." And he was as good as his word.

He retired from playing when I joined Barnsley Cricket Club. This was big news. This meant I was definitely going to play for Yorkshire and England. It didn't work out that way, but we had fun trying.

He used to stand by the sightscreen and watch every ball I faced and if the bat wasn't straight, if there was a gap between bat and pad, and particularly if I exhibited too soon in my innings my love of the cut he would semaphore his displeasure from the sidelines. He was demonstrating my lack of technique in one game when the stumper said to me: "Are tha' watching what I'm watching?" I said I was. "I reckon he's having a bloody fit," said the stumper. Then he said: "Does tha' know him?" "Never met him before in my life," I said.

I received an invitation to go to the Yorkshire nets for a trial, but I wasn't good enough. Maurice Leyland was coaching and he took one look at my late cut and sorrowfully shook his head. They liked the guy I was opening with at that time, Dickie Bird. He went on to play for Yorkshire.

And then, in my last season at the Club before I came South, another lad got the nod. He was Geoffrey Boycott. They sent the telegram on to the field to tell him he was to report to Headingley the next day. He declared his innings closed and walked from the field. The opposing skipper asked for an explanation. "I've finished with this sort of cricket," said Geoffrey Boycott. And he had.

When I gave up playing for Barnsley I told my dad that instead of being Len Hutton I was going to try to be like Neville Cardus. This pleased him because he was a Cardus fan. That didn't happen either, but by this time he was concentrating on plotting a way for his grand-child to be born in Yorkshire.

I had been living in Manchester when Mary became pregnant and had come to a very pleasant arrangement with the National Health Service in that splendid town.

Shortly before Mary was due to have the child I was offered a job in Fleet Street and we decided that we would leave the hospital

arrangements as they were rather than Mary travel to a hospital in London.

One day I received a phone call from my father: "Job's done," he said. "What job is this?" I asked. "I've shifted Mary to a nursing home in Wakefield," he said. "Why?" I asked. "Why?" he said, as if I was barmy. "What happens if it's a boy and it's born in Lancashire?"

I didn't ask him how he knew it would be a he, or what he might do if it wasn't. When my son was born my father suggested he be called Frederick Illingworth Parkinson in honour of Yorkshire's two great bowlers. We called him John after my father instead. He didn't play for Yorkshire either.

Just before he died I was talking to my father and he said that I had had a fortunate life being able to meet my heroes and write about sport. And then he said to me: "But you know, lad, none of it is like playing cricket for Yorkshire is it?" And I had to agree.

If you heard a noise the other day when Yorkshire decided to change the rules it was my father turning over in his grave. And given that what I have just described of growing up in Yorkshire was an even stronger part of his heritage it would be amazing if he hadn't moved.

But things are different now. It's all changed and if the club doesn't then it is doomed.

The fact is even with an overseas player fathers will still take their pregnant wives to the county. It is part of the folklore of being Yorkshire. The White Rose will always mean something special in cricket whether worn by a man born in Barnsley or one in Bangladesh because it was once the most feared and respected emblem in all the cricketing world.

That's what I think. But I'm dreading what the old man is going to say to me when next we meet. Not to mention Lord Hawke.

NEWS ITEM: Last week Michael Parkinson's World XI, captained by Gordon Greenidge, played India at the Scarborough Cricket Festival. Mr Parkinson, described as a "television personality", is thought to be the only man to have appeared on Jim'll Fix It and in Wisden.

Mr Parkinson was also President of this year's Festival. There are unconfirmed reports that Lord Hawke has turned over in his grave.

When I first started going to the Scarborough Cricket Festival as a child, I was fascinated by H D G Leveson Gower's XI. He was the only man I knew of who owned his own cricket team. Where, I wondered, did he keep them in the winter?

In those days I knew two things for certain. The first was that I would never bring my own cricket team to the Scarborough Festival. The second was that I would meet Fred Astaire.

That I have done both only highlights life's glorious uncertainty, and underlines the power of prayer. I was so fascinated by Mr Leveson Gower that I went looking for him. Forty-odd years ago people who had their own cricket team would stay at the Grand Hotel, which was very grand, but today is owned by Butlin's.

I used to work at the Grand. My uncle was a chef there and during the summer holiday I used to peel potatoes for pocket money. I peeled so many it is likely that if you had a potato at the Grand recently it was one of mine.

What is certain is that Mr Leveson Gower and his team ate the fruits of my labour. I only mention this because while waiting outside the Grand in the hope of meeting Mr Leveson Gower I had to invent an introductory gambit. I decided upon: "Good evening sir, you don't know me but you just ate my Jerseys." Or something like that. Fortunately, for both of us, we never met.

Cricket festivals have been sad casualties of the changes in our cricket calendar. There are still cricket weeks, but only Scarborough remains as a celebratory festival.

It is more than 100-years-old and now stands alone as a reminder of a different time when the proper finale to a season was a place with flags and buntings, and brass bands playing all day long.

Preserving the Scarborough Festival is not easy. Fortunately, for all who love the tradition of cricket, there are enough determined and dedicated men at the Scarborough club to keep it vigorous for a few years yet.

I love the Festival because it reminds us of the most important lesson of all, that when you strip away the politics and the aggravation and the tabloid headlines about who is doing what to who and why, what you are left with is a game. Simply that.

But it is more than that too. It is a game of character and humour, and a festival is a reaffirmation of cricket's qualities.

In the early days, I watched Fred Trueman running into bowl in time to the brass band playing selections from HMS Pinafore. In those days, the band played all-day long.

Once, during an economy drive, it was decided to dispense with the band and employ an organist. He had just started "I Do Like To Be Beside The Seaside" when he was forced to flee by a group of outraged purists.

Apart from the music, the other sound particular to the Festival used to be the mid-afternoon mock gun battle fought on the nearby lake.

I was watching one afternoon when Ray East was bowling. As he moved into his delivery stride, there was the sound of cannon-fire whereupon Mr East collapsed in front of the startled umpire as if he had been shot.

It is impossible to remain straight-faced for too long at Scarborough. The setting and the hospitality won't allow it. It brings out the best in people. It can make strong men wax lyrical.

For instance, it was at a Scarborough Festival that I once sought out Fred Trueman to ask him for a quote on the state of Yorkshire cricket at the start of the county's decline, before any of us had begun to feel downhearted about it.

Pervading optimism and the joys of the Festival had put Fred in good humour. "The future of Yorkshire cricket, ah?" he mused.

"Take this down," he instructed. I held my pen at the ready. "Yorkshire cricket will not be in decline for much longer," he said.

I made an appreciative grunt. He searched around for the telling quote and said: "In my opinion, very shortly Yorkshire cricket will arise like a Spartacus from the ashes."

Walking along the sea front I was delighted to observe the continuing popularity of beach cricket. Scarborough was my favourite pitch, though my father, who dedicated his life to a study of these things, told me that Filey beach was the best wicket in Yorkshire.

Those of you who believe that beach cricket is a jolly romp would have found no place in my father's team. He approached our matches in an entirely scientific manner, employing tidal charts and weather forecasts in his game plan.

Once he had the necessary information, he would search the beach for opponents, preferably holidaymakers from Lancashire, and invite them for what they imagined to be a friendly knockabout on the sands. What they did not realise until it was too late was that they were involved in the seaside equivalent of a Test match.

He would start the game just after low tide and invite our opponents to bat first. They accepted this as a sporting gesture from a chivalrous opponent affording them first use of a virgin strip of sand that was bound to cut up rough as the game progressed.

Thus lulled, they would be allowed to bat for an hour or so unaware that my father was more concerned with the state of the incoming tide than the number of runs they scored.

When their turn to field came, and square leg felt the sea lapping around his ankles, they began to have the feeling that all was not as it should be.

Panic would set in when the water reached knee level, and the well-placed hook shot meant an all-run 20 while the fielder waited for the ball to return on the incoming tide.

There were the more determined souls who set off in pursuit across the North Sea and tested the efficiency of the local lifesaver, but more often than not our opponents would concede the game knowing they had been outwitted by one of beach cricket's great tacticians.

When my father gave up beach cricket, we had not been defeated in 10 seasons. He did not retire. Word got around and he ran out of opponents.

There was one day during this year's Festival that approached

perfection. In the morning with the sun up, I played golf at Ganton, which is everything a golf course should be and even more. I missed a tiddler on the 18th and the match was halved.

I arrived at the ground and watched the cricket, with Richardson and Greatbatch playing glorious strokes.

I looked at the scoreboard which announced: Michael Parkinson's World XI versus India. I thought that in 100 years' time, some child will pick up a Wisden and wonder what manner of man was this who had his own cricket team, much as I had wondered about Mr Leveson Gower.

At that moment my reverie was interrupted by a youth carrying an autograph book. "Excuse me," he said, "are you Barry Norman?" It is a small price to pay for immortality.

I used to dream of going to Australia. My father told me that if he won the pools he would take me there. He never got lucky, but I did. Sadly he had died by the time I could afford the air tickets. He wanted to sit on the Hill at Sydney and give the Aussies what for. I went on his behalf and sat there for both of us thinking how he would have relished the mateyness of the Aussie spectators and their love of an argument.

My father firmly believed that Australians and Yorkshiremen were of the same tribe. Sworn enemies, yet blood brothers.

I once sat with him at Bradford in 1948 when Bradman's seemingly invincible team came nearer to defeat than at any other time on the tour.

The star of the game was Keith Miller. He won the match with his bowling and in the first innings made the highest score in grand style while the rest fooled about. I asked my father what he thought of Miller. "I wish he played for us," he said.

It was after seeing him in the flesh that I put a photograph of Miller in my wardrobe opposite a picture of Betty Grable wearing a white swimsuit.

One day I saw my father looking at my collection of pin-ups. "They ought to get married them two and come and live round here," he said.

He was of the opinion that a son born of that liaison might have Miller's shoulders and Miss Grable's legs and would make a fine quick bowler.

He was not to know, and nor could I have imagined, that Keith Miller would become my friend and my guide in Australia. I first met him when we both worked for the Daily Express and were required to play an annual cricket match against our arch rivals, the Daily Mail.

Miller had little or no interest in the contest because he never enjoyed taking candy from children.

However, bribed by the promise of a good pub lunch and a 'phone line to his bookie, he was persuaded to turn out.

It was after a liquid lunch that I happened to be standing next to my hero in the slips. He was only bothering to keep his eyes open because he had his own tic-tac man who would appear at regular intervals and signal the news from Wincanton.

Thus I was crouched as our fast bowler thundered in, while Miller stood, hands in pockets, gazing towards the pub. The batsman nicked the ball which came swiftly to my right. I was thinking about a dive when Miller swooped to his left, completed a somersault and handed me the ball, saying: "I wonder what won that bloody race?"

When I first visited Australia in the late Seventies, it was Miller who had the idea of inviting me to lunch to meet a few 'fair dinkum' Aussies who didn't mind having a beer and a yarn with a Pom. I arrived at Miller's club to find that the table consisted of Raymond Russell Lindwall, Jack Fingleton, Neil Harvey, Arthur Morris, Alan Davidson, Bill O'Reilly and Harold Larwood. I thought I had died and gone to heaven. In fact, when I die, and if I go to heaven, I want the same dining arrangements.

Our lunch became an annual event, with sadly decreasing numbers. Fingo died. I miss him still. Ray Lindwall isn't too special; even the indestructible Nugget is a bit frail. But he's not lost his zest for life nor his capacity to talk a leg off an iron pot when the mood takes him.

I just listen. Miller about Arthur Morris: "I once bowled him eight bouncers in an over.

"There had been a lot of discussion in the press about short-pitched bowling. There was a lot of talk about banning it or limiting the number of bouncers so I thought I'd have a spot of fun.

"When Arthur came out to bat I put nine men on the square-leg boundary and came off my long run and just bowled at his head. When I bowled the first one Arthur said: 'Oh dear, a bouncer'. And every time I bowled another he'd say 'Oh my God, he's done it again'. And it so tickled me that I started laughing so much that the tears were running down my face as I came into bowl. I could hardly make it to the crease. Old Arthur was in a right state."

"Was Morris all right?" I enquired.

"All right?" said Miller, "he hit me for 34 in the over."

Fingleton on Larwood: "He was the greatest fast bowler I saw. He was so accurate and he skidded the bouncer."

Larwood on Fingleton: "He wasn't the greatest bat I bowled against but he might have been one of the bravest. You could hit him all right, but he wouldn't go down."

O'Reilly on Larwood: "He was an exceptional bowler. I remember going out to bat against him in a Test match when he had our batsmen hopping.

"My skipper told me: 'Just stay there!' I was midway through my backlift when the first ball flew past me. It was then that I decided discretion was the better part of valour and I retreated to square-leg which gave me a perfect view of what happened next. Larwood bowled a ball of such exceptional pace that it struck my bail and reduced it to a small pile of sawdust."

O'Reilly is allowed this story because he is Irish.

Fingo on opening for his club with the legendary Charles Macartney: "As he walked to the wicket, he said to me: 'Now think on, young Fingleton, be ready first ball'. I would have done anything for him but I wasn't sure what he meant. Did he mean be prepared for a quick single? Was he telling me to concentrate from the first moment?

"All these questions were racing through my mind as the fast bowler raced in for the first ball and as he did I saw Macartney walking down the wicket with his bat at shoulder level.

"In an instant several things happened. The bowler bowled and Macartney, halfway down the wicket, gave it an awesome smack. The bowler dived for cover, so did I. The ball hit the sightscreen on the full and bounced back 50 yards on to the field of play.

"It was the most audacious shot I have ever seen. As I lay there alongside the fast bowler, who was by now a gibbering wreck, I looked up and saw the batsman standing above me tapping the wicket with his bat. 'Just like I said, young Fingleton. Always ready from the first ball'. He looked at the hapless bowler: 'They don't like it you know,' he said, confidentially."

Lovely Jack. I did a couple of television shows with him in Australia and people demanded more. We persuaded him back for the third time but it worried him. He didn't think he could deliver again. Late at night, before the recording, he rang me: "I don't know what to do that will be different."

I tried to placate him. "Jack, you'll think of something," I said. He called back an hour later: "I've been pondering what you said and I think I have the answer," he said.

"What is it?" I asked.

"Ever had anyone croak on your show?" he asked.

Before he died he gave me his first Australian cap. Three years ago Keith Miller gave me his last Australian sweater. They have all given me much else besides.

What sums up Australia for me and why I can't wait to get out there again was a dinner I went to in an outback town during the last England tour.

I was asked to make a speech but as the time approached for me to sing for my supper it became apparent that proceedings were out of hand. The assembly was noisy and drunk and not about to be quiet to listen to another whingeing Pom.

The man introducing me tried hard to appeal for calm but with little effect. In desperation he tried his trump card: "Come on guys give the Pom a go," he said. "After all, it'll be better than a poke in the eye with a burnt stick."

It was then I knew I had found my second home.

It is quite by chance that my chosen reading for the Melbourne Test was *Can't Anyone Here Play This Game!* The sentiment must have crossed Graham Gooch's mind more than once as he saw his batsmen give their wickets away. The book, in fact, is one of my favourite sporting stories. It is the account by Jimmy Breslin of the first year in the history of the New York Mets when the team created a reputation, unsurpassed before or since, of being the worst baseball team there has ever been. So bad that Casey Stengel, the legendary manager, who had seen most things in his long and successful career, was moved to utter the immortal words that form the title of the book. The Mets were so bad and, as Breslin states, so adept at snatching defeat out of the jaws of victory, that the fans took to them in a big way. They became an institution and the only problem they faced as the season progressed was that they might hit a winning streak.

In a team of no-hopers one man stood out. He was Marvin Throneberry, known as Marvellous Marv, whose lack of talent on the field was matched by his inability to handle the entire business of living. For instance, having been persuaded by his fan club that he was a star and therefore worthy of a rise in pay, he decided to face the awesome Casey Stengel with his request.

After much rehearsing of what he was going to say he finally plucked up courage to confront the manager. He burst into the office and slammed the door behind him so hard that the door knob came off in his hand. Sadly Mr Stengel was not in his office and Marvin had to be rescued via a window by the New York Fire Brigade.

On another occasion Marvin was invited by his fan club to a dinner in his honour. Upon arriving at the restaurant he discovered so many people there that he couldn't get in and he had to eat across the street where he could at least hear the crowd enjoying itself on his behalf.

Breslin's book is a delight. Not just because Breslin is a marvellous writer – Dick Schaap, who contributes the foreword to the book, describes Breslin as "writing out of the side of his mouth" – but

because it is a reminder of a time when sport was fun even when your team were losing.

I do recommend the book. You don't lend it to friends. It is the sort of book you never get back. I lost five copies like that and the only way I might be persuaded to part with this one is to give it to Graham Gooch to see if he laughs and also to persuade him that there is always someone in the world worse off than you are.

Whenever I see Mervyn Hughes I am reminded of Marvin Throneberry. I am not suggesting Merv is the worst cricketer in the world, indeed he is a good player. It is just that there is something vulnerable and slightly comical about the man. "Merv Mania" is not as rampant as it was a year ago but it is still going strong enough to earn him a place in the list of top 50 money-earners in Australian sport.

The difference between Merv and Marv, of course, is that one is presented via the imagination and talent of a wonderful journalist and the other is beamed directly at us by television. I imagine that before television a Robertson-Glasgow or a Cardus would have had great fun with Merv Hughes.

The trouble with television when it dictates a sport, as with cricket in Australia, is that the nuance of character like Hughes becomes overwhelmed by the blatant projection of what is considered a commercial image. This can be the only excuse for Merv's moustache. At present it is so large and severe that it looks like his face has been clamped. The Mervyn Hughes Lookalike Competition is in grave danger of collapsing because no-one can invent a moustache more ludicrous than the one they are supposed to parody.

But with or without disguise he is the sort of sportsman who attracts good stories. My favourite Merv tale is when he was having a terrible time in Australia and arrived at the third Test in Adelaide having taken one wicket in the series. In the middle of one unproductive spell a spectator shouted: "Hughes, you're useless."

This continued for a while and Merv did not respond until the barracker changed his tack and shouted "You can't bowl Hughes. How many wickets have you taken this series?" Merv lost his temper and gave the spectator two fingers, whereupon his tormentor bellowed: "And you can't bloody count either."

B ill O'Reilly recently had one of his legs amputated below the knee. It means, he tells me, that he will no longer be able to operate from his full run but otherwise he is bearing up.

He is in his eighties and neither cruel illness nor old age can change his feisty manner. He is a mettlesome man, full of opinion and argument. When I called to inquire about his condition he said: "I just sit here watching the kitchen wall in case someone runs off with it. It is a very boring occupation but I have to tell you that it is infinitely more interesting than watching one-day cricket."

For 13 years, O'Reilly has been an implacable enemy of the pyjama game and an outspoken critic of the razzamatazz surrounding it. He treats any attempt to persuade him of the game's virtues with a contemptuous snort. And yet there is little doubt that in his pomp he would have been the perfect one-day bowler. He spun the ball from leg at little under medium pace, he made it bounce, he had perfect control and a fearsome competitive spirit, hence the nickname "Tiger".

After he retired from cricket he kept a critical eye open as a journalist and his opinions were what you might expect from a man who bowed to no-one, including Don Bradman. Shortly after our conversation, a friend of mine persuaded him to be guest of honour at a luncheon in the company of Ray Lindwall, Neil Harvey, Arthur Morris, Norman O'Neill, Rod Marsh, Alan Davidson, Mike Gatting, Godfrey Evans, Martin Donelly, Bill Brown, Alec Bedser and Ken Archer.

O'Reilly, in full flow, was asked about the modern curse of "sledging" opponents. "Never spoke to an opponent on the field of play," he said, "except on one occasion when an English batsman called me a cheat."

"Then what?" I inquired.

"It didn't happen again, that's what," said O'Reilly, with an enigmatic smile.

Someone reminded him that in the Sixties, when commenting on the Australian v West Indies series, he supported Charlie Griffith when the fast bowler ran out Ian Redpath, who was backing up, without first warning him. He still thinks he was right, that any batsman seeking to take unfair advantage of a bowler deserves all he gets.

But he was reminded that during the Griffith row he was taken to task by his good friend, Jack Fingleton, who accused him of being provocative and asked what he would have done in a similar situation. The question was fanciful, said O'Reilly. "How so?" inquired Fingleton. "Because," said Tiger with a twinkle, "when I was bowling, the non-facing batsmen were never that eager to get down the other end."

I watched part of the Sydney Test with Raymond Russell Lindwall. He had just been interviewed at some length for the national sound archive. I'll bet we don't ask Fred Trueman to do the same. But we ought to.

I think Lindwall was the greatest fast bowler that I ever saw. I can still picture him clearly, warming up as the fielders fanned out behind the bat. His action is imprinted in my memory like the footprints he left in soft English turf.

When he bowled at my hero, the great Len Hutton, I could hardly bear to watch. But, worst of all, even if Len and I survived the first over, we knew that Keith Miller was to follow. There has never been a more devastating nor more contrasting pair of bowlers. Lindwall glided to the wicket like a man on castors; Miller rampaged in, hair flying, nostrils flaring.

I reminded Ray of the 1948 tour and the innings played by Hutton at the Oval when England were bowled out for 52, Lindwall taking six for 20 and Hutton scoring 30. What I wanted to confirm was that it took the best catch ever taken by a wicketkeeper to dismiss my hero. "What do you think happened?" asked Ray.

"Well, you bowled to Len, who glanced you off the full face of the bat and it looked a certain four until Don Tallon dived yards to his left and held the ball, one-handed, inches above the turf."

Lindwall nodded. "Now I am going to tell you what really happened," he said. "Len nicked the ball on to his pad which slowed it down sufficiently for Don to dive across and take the catch. Oh, and by the way, it was my slower ball otherwise even if it had nicked the pad it would have been four," he said.

To think that for 40-odd years I have been playing that memory at the wrong speed.

There is little doubt that the Australian television coverage of the Test matches is technically streets ahead of anything British television offers. The same cannot be said about the commentary.

I have two main objections: the commentators talk too much; and much of what they say is twaddle. There are exceptions. They are called Richie Benaud and Geoffrey Boycott. Benaud has been perfecting his craft for years. Today he sets the standard for the rest to follow. Boycott, who has never been frightened of seeking good advice, is a willing pupil. There are one or two others who could do with a lesson.

Max Walker, for instance is an affable and talented man but I do wish that occasionally he would put a cork in it. I do not wish to be informed as a bowler walks back to his mark that his heart is pounding, his mouth is dry and he is wearing size 11½ boots.

Max, by the way, is indisputably clairvoyant. He tells us that, as the bowler approaches the wicket, he will already have licked his fingers and wrapped them around the seam prior to ripping them over the top of the ball to produce the perfect leg cutter.

Similarly the feuds between commentators – Greig needling Lawry, Chappell needling anyone within hailing distance – sound awkward and false, like theatrical contrivance. And here's the nub: the Aussies are not so much reporting the game as selling it like washing-up liquid.

They start with the premise that the viewer knows nothing other than the basic fact that one player throws a ball at another who tries to hit it with a piece of wood. There is nothing wrong with instructing the client providing that, after a while, you assume they have got the drift and are ready for a more sophisticated approach. Sadly, there is no room for nuance.

The producers work on the theory that if nothing is happening on the field of play – which is to say that the run rate has fallen below six an over – then the viewer must be protected from becoming bored by

a series of sideshows. These range from flogging books, to cutaways of pretty girls [known in the trade as 'crumpet shots'], to asking viewers to 'phone in an answer to the question of the day.

This last ploy gives a pertinent clue to the kind of thinking dominating the TV presentation. The two questions posed to viewers were: should umpires make use of television technology in making decisions and should Test matches be played under lights? In other words, should television be given an even firmer stranglehold on the future of the game?

The trouble with the big sell is that, generally speaking, it creates an appetite for a certain kind of cricket: confrontational, disputatious, muscular, uncomplicated. These characteristics have their place in cricket: think of Ian Botham.

What is missing are the ingredients that make cricket such a special game – elegance, grace, wit, even eccentricity: think of David Gower.

Most of all it denies the viewer those contemplative moments between overs when cricket lovers see the field as a chess board and ponder the next move. In Australia there is a commercial break at the end of every over. So it is possible to go from the glory of Mark Waugh's strokeplay straight to a commercial for cockroach repellent.

Amid much that is crassly commercial, it is remarkable that Messrs Benaud and Boycott manage to be intelligent, instructive, perceptive and, above all, properly neutral. So far Bill Lawry has refrained from appealing on behalf of the Australian bowlers, but only just. On the second day of the current Test match he did say: "That's out" when Graham Gooch was struck on the pad and before the umpire had time, quite properly, to turn down the appeal.

Mr Lawry reminds me of my old man who, when he stopped playing, did a bit of umpiring. It should be said that as a player he was an enthusiastic appealer. He was standing in a game when I was bowling and having hit the batsman on the pads with one that was going well down the leg side, I was astonished, as was the batsmen, to see the umpire leap in the air and yell "Howzat".

When my father realised he was the only person appealing he shook his head and said loudly: "Not out, you silly old sod".

What Richie Benaud has accomplished, and Boycott is moving towards, but most have yet to learn, is that while a camera might show you the face of cricket only a commentator can describe its true nature.

In case you suspect me of being biased towards Geoffrey Boycott, let me plead guilty to having been his friend for 30 years or more during which time he has annoyed and delighted me, caused me to nod my head in approval and shake it in despair, made me both happy and sad.

He would say the same about me. That is the way of friendships. When I first knew him he was aged 15 and a promising newcomer to the Barnsley side. At the time I was opening the innings with Dickie Bird. It is strange to think back to those days when we were all dreaming of playing for Yorkshire and to see what happened. Two of us accomplished the dream, and more. Boycott became one of the great batsmen, Bird one of the best umpires . . . and I was attacked by an emu. Such is fate.

The point is there was always rivalry between us in those days, and in the case of Geoffrey Boycott and me, it continues nowadays on the golf course. The first thing to be said about playing golf with him is that it takes a long time.

Our first contest took place in Australia a couple of years ago when, having taken $2\frac{1}{2}$ hours to play the front nine, I suddenly lost the will to live. As I recall it, I was holding the flag at the 10th while Mr Boycott prowled the green inspecting his putt from every angle when I came to the conclusion that my life was ebbing away and I was doing nothing more exciting than holding a flag for my friend to aim at.

I conceded the match and told Mr Boycott that while I admired what he did to the Aussies when he was playing, I did not approve of him doing the same to me on a golf course. He smiled that secret smile and took the money.

We played the return match at the Australian Golf Club. This is no ordinary course. Designed by Mr Nicklaus it is on the tough side of difficult. After six holes my opponent had dropped one shot and I was five down.

I did feel it my duty to inform Mr Boycott that making par was not obligatory, and he took notice because, at the turn, I was only three adrift.

Mr Boycott began to fall apart on the back nine and it was then that I was introduced to his Uncle Bertie. It would seem that Bertie is not much of a golfer for whenever he played a shot he was unhappy with Mr Boycott would say: "Even my Uncle Bertie could do better than that". Or: "I am playing like my Uncle Bertie."

I was two down with two to play when thunder and lightning caused us to abandon play. Mr Boycott claimed the match on the grounds that there was no way I would win the last two holes because I couldn't beat his Uncle Bertie.

Losing meant I paid for dinner. This is where my game plan for the return started. I reckoned if I could breach Mr Boycott's routine of a light meal, a glass of wine and an early night I might stand a chance on the morrow.

Not being a drinker, Mr Boycott doesn't know what he is drinking and, being a Yorkshireman, he has never looked a gift horse in the mouth. Therefore, when the restaurant owner offered him a complementary drink of black sambucca, he accepted without understanding the consequences. Anyone who has drunk black sambucca will know that it has to be approached with caution and kept from naked light. Mr Boycott had two or three and next morning wished he hadn't. I won 5 & 4 to square the series.

The decider will be played in England but Mr Boycott has decreed the venue must be at least 50 miles from the nearest Italian restaurant. I fear the worst. None the less he was philosophical in defeat, pointing out that he now knew he could not play golf with a hangover. I volunteered to show him how, but he declined.

We sat and drank mineral water and contemplated the scene. A breeze ruffled the eucalyptus trees, somewhere a kookaburra was having an argument with nature. Thirty-something years ago we sat in the pavilion at Barnsley not knowing where we might end up, except in the middle trying to make a name for ourselves.

I have measured out my life in cricket bats. Curiously enough the first I owned was a two-face one made from a neighbour's fence. It didn't have a sweet spot. I don't think they were invented in those days. It was as rigid and dead as a plank of wood, which is what it was.

If you made contact with a hard ball it sent shock waves through your body. You got pins and needles in the arms and your teeth rattled. It was a crude prototype of the new design to be set before the MCC for approval.

It was rejected by the players of the Barnsley and District Backyard League as soon as we found an alternative. This was provided by an evacuee from London who brought with him a Patsy Hendren autograph his dad had provided as soon as he discovered his son was being shipped to Yorkshire.

It was brown with age and linseed oil and half the blade had been sawn off to transform it into a junior bat. It was the only bat I played with which had a handle as long as the blade. Looking back it was also the only bat I can recall from my Yorkshire childhood that was not signed by Len Hutton.

No matter, the Patsy did us well. Our wicket was on a strip of land next to the chip shop and ideally placed to ambush the drunks as they lurched home from the boozer. Invariably they would stop to watch our game and, without exception, demand a bowl. We would bet them three pence that they couldn't bowl out one of us in 10 minutes and we rarely lost. The first five minutes would be fairly good natured, but then the thought of losing to a snotty-nosed kid with half a bat in his hand would accelerate their ambition. When this happened it helped to be able to play the bouncer, not to mention the beamer.

It taught us a lot about survival and even more about the wondrous effect 10 pints of Barnsley Bitter can have on the human imagination. When they arrived at our game they were colliers with a bag of chips, just this side of legless.

But as soon as they removed their coats and had the ball in their hands you could tell what they dreamed about. Not surprisingly most bowling actions resembled either Alec Coxon or Johnny Wardle, who were then Yorkshire's two best bowlers.

Coxon ran to the wicket with his right arm jerking up and down rather like a man blowing up a tyre with a hand pump. Wardle sidled to the wicket giving none of his intentions away. He was like a man lobbing a bomb into a room. I always thought he ought to be wearing a black cloak and mask.

There were a couple of our customers who modelled their actions on the Kent and England bowler D V P Wright. This is how I became acquainted with Mr Wright's action, some time before I saw him bowl. The first time I was convinced that the bowler was having a fit. It was only when I saw Mr Wright play that I realised it had been a fair imitation. It is difficult to describe his action, which was long and bounding and so packed with physical curlicues that you would not have been surprised had he finished off with a cartwheel.

In the main our opponents were easy pickings because their ambition exceeded their ability. The only man we feared was our local fast bowler Mr Baker, who had the longest run I have seen. Had he measured it out on our pitch it would have taken him across the road and halfway down our street.

His approach was smooth until halfway to the wicket when he would execute an extraordinary movement rather like a man doing a rumba. You half expected him to arrive at the crease with Carmen Miranda on his arm. However, it didn't do to mock Mr Baker because, unlike most of our customers, he knew how to bowl and, what is more, generally hit what he was aiming at.

I was just into my teens when I graduated from the strip by the chip shop into our local team. By this time I owned a proper bat. It had a Len Hutton autograph and a short handle and its purchase was not so much a business transaction as an initiation ceremony into manhood.

We bought it from the sports department at the local Co-op for £3 10s. The blade was creamy and it had a wide straight grain. I loved that bat more than any I possessed and it lasted from pubescence to the start of National Service. I cleaned it with a razor blade and protected it with linseed oil.

When it chipped and splintered at the edges I had it bound with string, and when there was more string showing than wood, I had a re-blade. I took it to my bedroom at night and practised forward defensive shots. I tried to copy my great hero Len Hutton, whose photograph was stuck on the inside of the wardrobe door. Aware, even in those innocent days, that someone might think this strange I glued a picture of Alice Faye next to Len.

I was only once unfaithful to my bat. That was when I was seduced by a flash number owned by Mr Stewardson, our big hitter. I was a nudger and a deflector and I always envied the way that Mr Stewardson could strike a cricket ball.

I had never seen a bat like his. The blade was covered by a dark brown hide kept in place by tacks up the back of the bat. It had a long handle and seemed to weigh a ton. Mr Stewardson used it like a club and when he connected the ball would threaten distant parishes. It was unlike any bat I have seen. There was something strange and mystical about it. I think that when he finished with it he threw it into a lake near Camelot.

I wanted a bat like it very badly and one day asked Mr Stewardson where I might buy one. He said I couldn't because there wasn't another bat like it in the world. "Does tha' want to know its secret?" he whispered. I nodded. He looked around to see that no-one was listening and then said, conspiratorially: "It's what the bat's covered in that meks t'ball go a long way. Does tha' know what it is?" I shook my head. He drew me close to his side and whispered: "Kangaroo skin."

I went to our sports shop but the man said someone was pulling my leg. I asked Mr Roberts, our other big hitter, if he had kangaroo skin on his bat. He said he didn't but confessed that the secret of his powerful hitting was that he used a 10-springer. I went back to the sports shop to order one. The man said he didn't have one in stock but he could sell me a left-handed cricket bat.

I dare not accuse Mr Roberts of pulling my leg. That would have been insensitive as he was one short of a pair in the leg department. Not that he ever made any concession to his impediment. Indeed he used it to his advantage. He never bothered to wear a pad on his tin leg so that when struck upon it there would be a noise like a bell chiming. If the bowler dare to shout "Ow's that?" the batsman would smile at him sweetly and say: "One of clock and all's well."

When next I changed my bat it was for a Gunn and Moore. This saw me through National Service and its cousins through the remainder of my career as a serious cricketer. The change to something more frivolous occurred when I started playing for various showbiz teams. By this time I had been reduced to accepting hand-outs from friends.

It therefore came to pass that using the same bat Geoffrey Boycott had scored 2,000 runs with – and by the look of it all off the middle – I topedged an underarm delivery from Barbara Windsor and was caught by Sue Lawley. Most shaming of all was when I went to the wicket carrying a bat presented to me by that most elegant and gifted of Australian players, Greg Chappell. He had used it to score a century against England. He signed it on the back and gave it to me to use in a charity raffle. I decided that before I let it go I would try it out, to see if it worked for me like it had for Greg. I dressed for the occasion: clean whites, spotless boots, buckskin pads (whatever happened to buckskin pads?). I took guard making sure the wicketkeeper saw the autograph on the back of the blade.

It was a showbiz game, but not in my head. I was at Lord's opening for England and Michael Holding was ghosting in towards me. The ball came through the air, red and gleaming. I saw it all the way. I took the toe to the line, swung my magic bat and hit a large and ripe salad tomato. Everyone thought it was hilarious. None of them knew the sacrilege that had been committed.

Nowadays I don't own a cricket bat. Instead I look with incredulity at the various shapes and sizes. I picked up one owned by my eldest son and I swear the handle was as far round as a drain pipe. They cost more than a hundred quid. You could have bought our field for that, plus the chip shop. The game is overwhelmed by technology with scoops and sweet spots and names like Jumbo and Powerdrive.

What seems to have been forgotten is that a cricket bat should be beautiful as well as practical, better designed as a baton than a cudgel. Last season I played in a game with a man who had a Patsy Hendren bat. It was the colour of old furniture and glowed with care. It was the brother to the one we used to play with all those years ago. When it struck the ball I swear it made a noise like a bass gong. It was the sort of bat you could have a conversation about, and we did. It had belonged to the batsman's father and was a family heirloom used only on special occasions.

It was a tribute to a craftsman's art, not like so much today, a product of commercial gimmickry.

I was 12 before they let me watch a Roses game. I had been to the cricket before – I had already seen such wonders as Constantine fielding, Compton batting and Miller bowling – but these were fripperies compared to the real thing.

Being allowed to go to a game between Yorkshire and Lancashire was an important ritual in growing up; like having your first pint or using a razor or wearing long pants.

My father took me to Bramall Lane in 1947 where we sat on the football terraces for the best part of the day through sunshine and rain, not daring to move but also not wanting to. There were 22,000 people in Bramall Lane that Saturday so long ago in conditions that nowadays would necessitate a public inquiry.

When my father stood up to go to the toilet he walked like Groucho Marx. Yet none of us would have swapped our concrete perch for a seat in Paradise that Saturday in August, 1947.

Yorkshire batted first. Hutton opened with Keighley who soon departed. Pollard and Phillipson were bowling well. The great Len was defending grimly and we settled down for a few hours of trench warfare. The crowd were happy.

This was Yorkshire v Lancashire and things were as they should be. Into the arena strode young Gerald Smithson. It was his first Roses game. He had already been given his instructions by Emmott Robinson who had told him to "stick thi' bat in t'block-hole and leave it there at all costs".

This was sound advice from one who knew. Instead, Mr Smithson played as if on the beach at Bridlington. He carted Phillipson for three fours and a three in one over. He was like a greyhound in a Donkey Derby. He missed his century by two runs but there will be those at Bramall Lane that day who still remember Smithson's 98 long after they have forgotten a dozen or more less dramatic centuries.

According to reports, the only person who was less than impressed by Smithson's innings was the aforesaid Emmott Robinson. As Smithson put Lancashire to the sword, Emmott was heard to mutter: "He'll nivver learn, yon lad; he'll nivver learn."

The contest was a draw, which is what was expected of Roses games in those days. It was not so much a cricket match as a ceremony between two great tribes.

Since my initiation, I have travelled far and wide, seen cricket in many countries and witnessed remarkable events, but none remain as vivid in my memory as the Yorkshire v Lancashire games of my youth.

Little did I know as I watched events unfurl at Bramall Lane there were one or two people on the field I would come to know in later life. If someone had told me that one day I would sit next to Len Hutton at dinner and talk about the art of batting I would have said they were mad. And yet I did.

Many years later I asked him what he thought of modern players. "Don't use their feet enough. They should watch Fred Astaire," he said.

I remembered this when I interviewed Mr Astaire. I wanted to tell him about Len Hutton but I thought it might confuse him, particularly as I would have to confess that when I saw him dance with Rita Hayworth in *You Were Never Lovelier* I could only compare it to Len Hutton's cover drive. Nor could I have known that Ellis Robinson, the Yorkshire off-spinner who all but did for Lancashire that day at Bramall Lane, was to be my team-mate at Barnsley three or four years later when he retired from county cricket.

I remember fielding for him in the leg trap when he was bowling at a slogger who cared little for reputation and whose only ambition was to kill forward short-leg.

As I retreated under the onslaught, Mr Robinson kept urging me closer. Finally I was struck a terrible blow on the kneecap and, as I lay on the ground in need of medical attention and sympathy, I was approached by the man responsible for my predicament.

I expected Mr Robinson to show some concern. Instead he stood over me and said: "Tha' stands abart as if thi' knickers were starched." I took it to mean that my wounds were self-inflicted. It was three years after Bramall Lane that I first visited Old Trafford. You must remember that in 1950 a journey from Barnsley to Manchester was like an adventure to another planet. It required all the planning of a space probe.

Our means of transport was an ancient Triumph motor car, lately acquired by my father, which had never been over the Pennines. It was a strange-looking contraption, mainly because it sloped.

This was because my father had replaced the springs at the rear of the car with some he had found in a scrapyard. I think they came from a double decker bus because they lifted the back so that the car appeared to be pointed downwards. Sitting in the back seat was a bit like being in a roller coaster on a steep descent.

I don't know what time we set off in the morning, but I do know it was dark. We arrived at Old Trafford at 7am by the time play started at 11.30 I had been up so long I was ready for bed. Lancashire had a new bowler playing in his first Roses game. Brian Statham was his name. "What's he like?" we asked our neighbours. They didn't know. But we soon found out.

He bowled Frank Lowson for a duck and did for Ted Lester in a similar fashion. Roy Tattersall dismissed Len Hutton and, before we knew it, Yorkshire were 40-odd for five and the young Statham had taken three for very few. It was our first view of that supple, whirling action which became the trademark of his quality. Did he ever bowl a long hop? I doubt it.

Norman Yardley rescued us that day with a century and once more the game was drawn. Statham apart, the significance of that trip was that it introduced me to Old Trafford and to Manchester, my favourite ground in my favourite northern city.

I also clapped eyes on Malcolm Hilton for the first time. Malcolm was a slow left-arm bowler who had achieved celebrity status by twice dismissing Don Bradman in 1948. This was an achievement comparable with having discovered penicillin and composed "As Time Goes By" on the same day.

I learned recently that he had died and I was greatly saddened because he was one of those rare men who cause you to smile at their memory.

He was a Lancashire hot pot of a man: his accent was plump and juicy; he had a tasty wit. He sometimes opened the bowling for Lancashire. Indeed, he did that day at Old Trafford against Yorkshire.

Those were the days when teams had spin bowlers instead of phantom seamers. He was a marvellous fielder, particularly close to the wicket, when Tattersall was bowling. Hilton, Ikin and Grieves didn't miss much in the leg trap.

But Malcolm's great gift was as a teller of tales. He was a droll with a faultless style. I once asked him about Tattersall and he said: "Tha could reckon he'd bowl one bad ball a year. I were t'spotter for t'leg trap. I fielded at backward short-leg so I could see where Tatt was going to pitch it. If it were short I'd shout 'duck lads!' and they'd know to get out of the way.

"One Pancake Tuesday Tatt bowled a long hop. I spotted it but I thought I'd have a bit of fun so I didn't call it. Well t'batsman got hold of it and gave t'ball a terrible thump. Tha' should have seen Jack Ikin's face. He didn't speak to me for three months."

"Did it hit him?" I asked. "No, he caught it," said Malcolm.

If ever a Lowry landscape needed a description then Malcolm Hilton's would have been the perfect voice. He ruminated on life with lugubrious wit. Anything would get him going.

I was sulking after missing a catch and he said: "One season I were in t'leg trap and were copping everything and Washy [Cyril Washbrook] says to me, 'Does tha' reckon thissen at cover, Malcolm'. And I said cocky as anything, 'Tha knows me skipper. I can catch 'em anywhere'.

"So I trot off to cover and this batsman gets reight under one from Tatt and up and up she goes until she's higher than Blackpool Tower and I'm running to get under her.

"Well I'd been runnin' like a stag for two minutes and she's still going up but now she's started drifting, going this way and that and I'm under her running round in circles thinkin' 'booger this'.

"And then t'bloody thing starts dropping and I'm still running all over t'place but now I'm shouting, 'it's mine, it's mine, it's mine', to get t'others out of the way.

"By this time I've got no idea where I am. All I know as t'ball gets nearer is I'm not properly under it so as it falls I dive forward. Next thing I know I've knocked down t'wicketkeeper, one set of stumps, two men in t'leg trap and t'umpire at square-leg. And I've still missed t'ball by 10 feet.

"So I'm lying theer among all t'debris – it were like a battlefield – and I look up and theer's t'skipper looking down at me. And he says, 'By the way Hilton, does tha' know any other daft tricks?'"

The character of men like Malcolm Hilton and Ellis Robinson was at the soul of the Roses games.

I haven't been to one lately because it has all changed – not just the cricket, but the rest of it. I listened to the radio commentary of last week's one day semi-final and was glad I wasn't there.

Not because Yorkshire lost but because, according to the commentators, there was ill feeling on the field.

One or two of the Lancashire players were petulant when Metcalfe was given not out and none of them applauded his century. This is not as it should be, and certainly not as it was.

What gave the Roses games their particular competitive edge was that each side had respect for the other. That might have disappeared and, if it has, the worse it is for players and spectators alike.

Tawdry behaviour is best forgotten. Not even a poet like Malcolm Hilton could incorporate it into the legend of Yorkshire v Lancashire.

If the modern players want a guide to what it used to be like, then let me tell him about Ken Taylor making his debut in a Roses game at Old Trafford in the 1960s. He went out to face a rampant Statham who had just dismissed two Yorkshire batsmen for no runs.

In those days there used to be a gate attendant at Old Trafford. As Ken walked out with the Lancashire crowd baying for blood the gateman said: "Good luck, young man. But think on, don't be long".

Ken was still pondering this instruction as Statham ran in and bowled him first ball. Ken walked back to the pavilion, whereupon the same attendant opened the gate, doffed his cap and said: "Thank you lad."

A cricket match, like a movie, is about moments. Whenever we think back to a particular game we don't remember every detail, only the significant events are locked in our memory.

I find that more often than not it is a catch or a particular piece of fielding I remember rather than a specific shot or a moment of bowling action.

I remember little of the very first time I visited Lord's shortly after the war, but I can see now Learie Constantine at coverpoint gliding across the turf, picking up and knocking the stumps down with his throw.

The batsman – I think it was Martin Donnelly – was not even within diving distance of his crease when Constantine hit the wicket. Not that batsmen dived for their crease in those days. Certainly not Martin Donnelly.

The last time I saw him he looked as elegant and stylish at 70-odd as he ever did in his 20s.

On one of my very first visits to Bramall Lane I saw Johnny Wardle catch Everton Weekes in the gully with such speed and lack of fuss that no-one in the ground knew what had happened until Weekes set off for the pavilion and Wardle picked the ball from his pocket and held it for the crowd to see.

Who were the best catchers? Philip Sharpe at slip took some beating. I think that he and Bobby Simpson were the two best slippers I saw. They both had the knack of seeming to catch the ball after it has passed them.

Fred Trueman had a great pair of hands close up or in the deep and Brian Close took more than his fair share of marvellous catches, many of them while standing so close to the batsman that they could have shared the same pair of trousers.

He was also the architect of one of the most extraordinary catches that never were. Fielding at forward short-leg he was struck a mighty blow on the forehead from a full-blooded pull shot, whereupon the ball rebounded to cover where a young Yorkshire colt was fielding.

Believing his skipper to be mortally wounded the colt ignored the rebound and ran to render first aid. His captain – who remained upright in spite of a blow that would have felled a normal ox and who now had a lump the size of an individual British Rail pork pie growing out of his forehead – put an end to the mission of mercy by bellowing: "Catch the bloody thing".

The young player, who was convinced that the blow had killed his captain and was not up to being bollocked by a ghost, suffered severe trauma and needed weeks of careful counselling to repair the psychological damage.

If we are talking about great fielders and the memories they give us, then I would have to put Derek Randall at the top of my list. No-one has given me more pleasure than Derek. Watching him prowl the covers, swooping, leaping, throwing has been one of the great delights of English cricket these past 20 years.

But there is more to Randall's fielding than skill; there is the celebration of being alive and playing the loveliest of games for a living; there is the enthusiasm for being paid to do something that you would willingly do for nothing; and there is in his joy and exuberance the clearest demonstration that at its best cricket is fun both to play and watch.

Not everyone appreciates Mr Randall's sense of humour. Notts were playing Yorkshire in a very tight game which John Hampshire was threatening to win. Bob White, the Notts spin bowler, set his field carefully, putting Randall by the sightscreen. He tossed one up to John who hit a soaring straight drive in the direction of Randall. The fielder stood under the ball until the last minute when he appeared to bow his head and let the ball fall behind him.

The umpire signalled six and White was halfway across the field to murder Randall when the fielder produced the ball from behind his back.

He explained that as he lined himself up he thought it might be fun to see if he could catch the ball if he put his hands behind his back. He did and the ball stuck. Had the ball gone for six and Notts lost the game it is doubtful if either White or Randall would have played the game again, but for very different reasons.

Let it be recorded that Michael Parkinson's Showbiz XI continued their unbeaten record by defeating Maidenhead and Bray by four runs.

This remarkable victory was achieved in the last over when a combination of Parkinson and Kenny Lynch dismissed the last Maidenhead batsman. The circumstances of the dismissal caused much debate among spectators and is likely to have a profound effect on the future of the game.

What happened was that captain Parkinson, a veteran of a thousand showbiz games, decided to bowl the last over in tandem with Mr Lynch. In other words, Mr Parkinson bowled over the wicket while, at the same time, Mr Lynch bowled round. The batsman, a Mr Cull, questioned the umpire about the legality of the tactic. Indeed, being an Aussie, Mr Cull put his argument most forcibly. This cut no ice with the umpire who is a friend and drinking companion of Mr Parkinson.

Mr Cull lasted three balls before being overwhelmed by superior tactics. The first two balls he faced, delivered simultaneously, were wide of the mark. Indeed, leg slip fielded one and backward point collected Mr Lynch's effort which, he claimed, was a late outswinger. Mr Cull managed to hit one of the next two balls hurled at him while the one he missed was taken by the 'keeper. It was now that Mr Parkinson's shrewd cricketing brain came into play and brought the game to an end.

Instructing Mr Lynch to bowl a slow, high full toss Mr Parkinson delivered at the same time a fast underarm delivery along the ground much in the manner of Trevor Chappell in that infamous incident against New Zealand. Thus it came to pass that Mr Cull was palpably lbw to the grubber and, even as the umpire raised his finger, was also bowled by the high full toss which fell out of the sun upon his wicket.

What happened at Maidenhead could have great significance to the game. If the England lads can slip the tactic past Dickie Bird and the rest, it could herald a bright new future for English cricket. Mind you, I don't know why Micky Stewart didn't think of it first. He is no stranger to showbiz cricket. Indeed, he was present at Edgbaston many years ago when I employed a similar tactic to dismiss Alvin Kallicharran.

On this occasion I worked out that for all his twinkling footwork, quick eye and whiplash wrists, he wasn't too good at playing the slow bouncer. I don't use the word 'bouncer' in the accepted sense of a ball whistling past a batsman's head. In this case 'bouncer' means a ball that bounces many times before it reaches the batsman.

Thus it was that I bowled Kallicharran with one that bounced three times. It was slow enough for Mr Kallicharran to have played at least three different strokes at it – including an off-drive and a sweep to leg – before it bowled him middle stump. Like Mr Cull, he was disappointed but forced to admit that he had been out manoeuvred by a superior cricket brain. Mr Stewart might argue that he has enough on his plate already without occupying his mind with such a radical reappraisal of tactics, yet, if truth be told, compared to organising a Showbiz XI, he has a bobby's job.

First of all the captain of a showbiz team can never assume that his players will turn up with the proper gear. Indeed, I once opened the innings with Jimmy Savile, who was wearing gold lamé trousers, purple boots and a sequined tee-shirt. He was smoking a cigar as long as his bat handle and had, I seem to remember, tartan hair.

In such circumstances the opposition must join in the fun, but on this occasion the opening bowler tried his hardest to hit Mr Savile between the eyes. I don't think Jimmy knew what was going on. I doubt if he saw the ball at all. After the third delivery had whistled past his ear I had words with the bowler.

"What are you trying to do?" I asked. "Knock his bloody head off," he said. "Why," I inquired. "Because my mother can't stand him on the telly," he said. When they talk about pressure I wonder if the likes of Graeme Hick really know what they're on about.

Again it is highly unlikely that Gooch, as captain, has the kind of problems I face every so often. For instance, I'll bet that he has never had his concentration broken by a visitor to the pavilion complaining that the ladies loos were overflowing.

The trouble with giving your name to a team is that you become the focal point for every complaint. Last week not only was I blamed for the toilets overflowing, but also for a traffic jam on the M4 and the sound system being a) too loud, and b) too quiet. I was accused of letting the commentator talk too much and too little, of allowing the beer tent to run out of booze and of not signing an autograph: "To Stephanie, Joyce, Syd, Darren, Tracey, Uncle Joe, Aunti Vi, Cousin Sharon, Tommy, Lucy, Dirk, Jo and Percy not forgetting all the lads in the snug at the Rat and Handbag, with much love and best wishes, Michael Parkinson. PS Arsenal for the Cup."

Apart from the fact it would have knackered me, I was at the time trying to convince one of my players that you strapped pads to the front of your legs and not on the sides as he was attempting to do.

I am still haunted by one incident with an autograph hunter. It was a long time ago in a charity game up north. During the tea interval I was alone in the pavilion after having taken a shower. I was naked and had my back to the door when I heard it open and someone enter. I assumed it was one of my team-mates. But then I heard a woman say: "Excuse me, Mr Parkinson, but could I have your autograph."

I looked for something to cover my nakedness and found a small towel, not big enough to go round my waist but just large enough to dangle in front of me like a sporran. When I turned I saw a most attractive young woman with a child of about five or six. Neither seemed the slightest bit embarrassed by the situation.

"Your autograph, please," said the woman, offering me her book. I said something silly like I didn't have a pen. She produced one and, by an extraordinary feat of contortion, I managed to sign her book while keeping the towel covering the area where normally my underpants would be . . . or so I thought.

I handed her the book. "Thank you," she said. "Say thank you to the nice man," she instructed the child who, throughout my ordeal, had stared unblinkingly at my semi-naked body. The woman started to leave and, as she reached the door, turned to me and with a sympathetic smile said: "Don't worry luv, I won't let on."

What did she mean? Did she see more than she was supposed to? If so, was her statement sympathetic or enigmatic? The memory echoes down the years and puzzles me still.

I sometimes wonder why I bother and then there is that moment when I lead the team on to the field and I know why. It is the knowledge that in all of sport no-one has been in charge of such a motley assortment of talent. In my time I have led on to the field at

Maidenhead and Bray such great players as Imran Khan, David Gower, Dennis Lillee and, this year, Gordon Greenidge. They have taken their place alongside the likes of Billy Connolly, Jimmy Tarbuck, George Best, Tim Rice, Annabel Croft, Lionel Blair, Alan Ball and Angela Rippon.

No captain in the history of the game has had so many tantalising options.

There was one slight hiccup this year. After proudly leading my team out I was approached by Mr Greenidge, who said politely: "Skipper, may I ask you who is keeping wicket?" What with the ladies' toilets overflowing and all the rest this minor detail had slipped my mind. Mr Greenidge himself donned the pads which was reassuring for me because I now spend my days in the field at first slip hiding behind the 'keeper.

For those who like details of play I must tell you that when we batted Mr Greenidge, after smiting one or two balls into the river, was bowled by our local dentist who now threatens to have a sign over the surgery door saying: "Have Your Teeth Pulled By The Hand That Bowled Gordon Greenidge."

It mattered little because a fighting 30-odd from George Best and a similar amount from Alan Ball took our total past 200.

It was in the field that my team best demonstrated its quirky qualities. Lionel Blair, fielding at fine leg, was a revelation. He approached the ball with a buck and wing and his return to the 'keeper was sometimes accompanied by a superb entrechat which drew cries of pleasure from the many balletomanes in the lager tent.

In the main the damage was done by Kenny Lynch and George Best. Mr Lynch has both a long run and a short run to the wicket and is the only bowler I know who is considerably slower off his long run. This could account for the bafflement he caused among the batsmen. Mr Best, on the other hand, is a mean bowler for someone who has played about half a dozen games in his life. When he left the field he was surrounded by children, none of whom were born when he was in his pomp. The remarkable thing about the man is that he remains a hero to a hearsay generation as well as to those who were fortunate enough to watch him in all his glory. One child said: "George, were you better than Paul Gascoigne?" George laughed. "Ask me, son," I said.

It was a lovely day for a cricket match in the most enchanting of

settings. In the evening, as the shadows lengthened, a band played and the setting sun glowed against the church tower. The flags on the marquees stirred in an evening breeze and the ladies loo was still over-flowing. It had been in all its beauty and its eccentricity a very English kind of day.

I was talking to a chap the other day who was going on about the state of sport in our schools. He was making the point that at present the education system was doing for British sport what Dutch Elm disease did for our landscape.

In many schools sports like cricket are not being taught any more, in some instances even if teachers wanted to teach a sport they couldn't because the playing fields have been sold off.

I started thinking if that had happened at my school I wouldn't have bothered turning up. I learned two skills at Barnsley Grammar School: how to smoke and how to play cricket. Both have proved lifelong afflictions.

In those days, before the educational theorists got to work, competitive sport was an important part of the school curriculum. It would have been easier for the headmaster to fire the Latin master than get rid of our sports teacher. To win your colours at either cricket or soccer was to become a god.

I regarded academic subjects as being what we did in between the periods set aside for games. So did many of my friends, and, I suspect, one or two of our teachers.

Mr Swift, who taught cricket, soccer and maths, was renowned for gazing longingly towards the cricket field while teaching algebra on a summer's day and could easily be deflected from a lecture on geometry by the proposition that if Pythagoras was alive and playing for Yorkshire he would bowl seam up like Mr Coxon, not leg breaks and chinamen like Mr Wardle. Webb Swift and my father were the two men who most influenced the way I played and thought about cricket. There was no conflict in philosophy between them.

They were both Yorkshiremen of a certain generation reared on the principles that batting was based on sound defence, bowling was a side-on art and cricket was a game best played in clean boots.

When I played my first net for Mr Swift I knew he was inspecting my father's handiwork. After 10 minutes the nod of the head meant

he was satisfied, as my father knew he would be. When people spoke of the Yorkshire system it was this continuum from family to teacher to club to county that was at the heart of it all. From our school playing field we could look down at the home of Barnsley Cricket Club. If Webb Swift did his job that would be the next step.

He was a stern teacher. He was a purist and a puritan about the game. As batsmen we were taught to play in the V. The bat must never move out of the perpendicular. Anything involving the bat moving out of a straight line was something you did later in life and only then if the ball was presented to you on a silver platter sitting up on a pile of cabbage.

If he had a fault it was that he could never comprehend that now and again he would come across a child so swift of eye and reflex that he demanded licence within the framework of the coaching.

Such a one was Hector, a chubby and lumbering youth who was one of the best strikers of a cricket ball I have ever seen. He played like a young Colin Milburn with a long free swing of the bat and a natural timing. He murdered schoolboy bowling yet could never convince Webb he was anything other than a chancer and, what was worse, a heretic.

The conflict between them came to a head during the Masters' versus Boys' game when Webb bowled and Hector smashed him out of sight. Every time Hector came down the track and crashed him straight into the distant soccer pitch for six Webb would shake his head sorrowfully and say: "Nay Hector lad, that's not the way to do it. Play it like this," and he would demonstrate a dead bat forward defensive shot.

Then Webb would bowl it a bit quicker and shorter, pushing it through and Hector would lay back and smack the ball past old-fashioned point. Webb would be almost weeping with frustration. "Hector, Hector, how many times must I tell you lad. When it's pitched there tha' does this", and he would demonstrate lifting an imaginary bat above his head to enable the ball to pass safely through to the wicketkeeper.

And so it continued until Hector mistimed a hit and long on caught him on the edge. He'd made 80-odd in no time and destroyed the bowling, particularly Webb's. But it didn't alter a thing. As Hector departed Webb Swift said to him: "I warned you, Hector lad. That's what slogging gets you."

He was aided in his search for perfection by the groundsman, Mr Matthewman, who produced the best batting strip I have ever played on. Like most groundsmen, given the choice, he would have preferred that we looked at his masterpieces rather than trod on them.

He regarded cricketers as heathens who scarred his work. Our fast bowler was called Wilson and he developed a pronounced drag in his delivery stride which ploughed a furrow you could plant turnips in. He turned up one day with a metal plate welded to his dragging toe cap in the manner of his great hero, F S Trueman. When he finished bowling it looked as if he had approached the wicket on a tractor. He was sent home before the groundsman saw the damage and murdered him with his reinforced footwear.

You had to play for the first team to get the chance to perform on John Matthewman's square. All other games were played on the outfield. When he had finished cutting and rolling the pitch he would take a razor blade and, on hands and knees, go in search of any errant weed or tumor. He sought perfection, and often achieved it. He hated fast bowlers, so he set out to break their hearts, and he sometimes did.

When I left school and went across the way to join the men at Barnsley Cricket Club, John Matthewman followed soon after and we had the best batting wicket in the Yorkshire League, including Headingley and Bramall Lane. Ask Dickie Bird or Geoffrey Boycott. They'll tell you the same. Looking back to my schooldays I only care to remember what happened on the playing fields. The rest was a waste of time. I spent a while trying to remember what I did at school when I wasn't being taught cricket by Webb Swift and the answer was being taught soccer by Webb Swift.

He had been a semi-pro with Halifax, I think – but whereas his love of cricket was based on its subtle and profound mysteries, his relationship with soccer was much more direct.

As a centre half he believed that football was a simple game played by simple-minded people. That being the case, "get stuck in" and "get rid" was about as deep as he intended to go when asked to elaborate his theory. He had no time for "fancy" players and would reward their ambitions with a swift kicking.

He was, of course, in the great tradition of Barnsley defenders like Skinner Normanton (whom God preserve) and epitomised by the great pre-war trio of Harper, Henderson and Holley. Old Tom Holley became a journalist when he stopped kicking people for Barnsley and Leeds and I used to sit next to him in the press box where he would upbraid me for extolling the virtues of the great Skinner.

"He were soft compared to them at Barnsley when I played theer," said Tom. Then he'd get all misty eyed as he remembered the havoc he'd caused: "Ay, 'arper, 'enderson and 'olley. Not much escaped our clutches, I can tell you," he said.

It might have been Tom, or if it wasn't it was someone else who wore the No 5 shirt at Barnsley, who would greet the opposing No 9 with the words: "Before we start tha's got a choice. Barnsley Beckett Hospital or Sheffield Royal Infirmary."

Barnsley crowds appreciated raw meat. As children they were reared on it through contact with teachers like Webb Swift. Whereas I won his approval by my dogged approach to batting I also incurred his wrath by my delicate manner on a soccer field. I never cared for the crunch of physical battle and I think Mr Swift had me down as a bit of a nancy.

It was therefore as spectator and not participant that I watched another Masters' versus Boys' match which featured a clash between Mr Swift and a young man called Duncan Sharpe. Duncan didn't need any coaching from Webb Swift.

When he arrived at Barnsley Grammar School he was a fully-fledged assassin of ball-playing forwards. He had a tackle like forked lightning and the build and constitution of a fighting bull.

It was inevitable that, having disposed of most of the Masters' forward line, he would eventually come face to face with Webb. They went for a 50-50 ball and, with a terrible clash of studs and bone, burst through the ring of watching spectators and slid down the bank on to the school playground.

When they stood up they both looked like they had been involved in a bad road accident; but the two of them were laughing. I knew then that Duncan Sharpe would play for Barnsley. And he did. During the time he wore the No 5 shirt it was said that certain centre forwards of nervous disposition were known to take sick with a mysterious illness just before they faced Duncan Sharpe at Oakwell.

You could argue that my education was a touch lop-sided. But no more so than those children who, for one reason or another, are nowadays denied a playing field or a sports master. And at least, in my day we had a choice. What is sad about today's set-up is that it has no place for the Webb Swift's of teaching.

Where they flourish still is where they always have and always will, at the public schools. Down the road at the state system the discrepancy between those who pay for their children and those who don't becomes more and more apparent.

It's not fair and it doesn't make sense. We should seek out our politicians and tell them so. But we won't. We've always had a nonchalant attitude towards sport, which is why our schools are in the state they are. Every Wimbledon we bellyache about our tennis players without doing anything about a system which would require a miracle to produce a winner.

I have never doubted the importance of sport in the education of the child. As I sit here writing this article I am reminded that though judged by academic standards my five years at Barnsley Grammar School were a complete waste of time, what I did learn there has enabled me to earn a living while pretending to be working.

In other words the job is the hobby and the hobby the job. I can't think of a better preparation for life than that. Can you?

NEWS ITEM: "Barnsley Cricket Club, who number Geoffrey Boycott, Dickie Bird and Martyn Moxon among their former players, may be forced to leave their ground midway through next season. The lease under which they have paid a peppercorn rent for over 50 years expires on August 1 and the owners of the ground, a local charitable trust, have offered a new three-year lease at £22,750 a year. A spokesman for the Trust said: 'We have sympathy with the club but we have been advised by the Charity Commission that we have to obtain the best possible income for the charity for the nine acres of land near the centre of Barnsley'".

Sounds ominous. Nine acres near the middle of Barnsley. Make a lovely car park, or a hypermarket, or a car park for a hypermarket. Whatever happens, you can bet any money that it won't be what it has been these past 50 years or more: a proper cricket ground. It wasn't some odd patch of grass on which cricket was played or an acre or two of grazing pasture with a wicket on it.

It was, and is, a real cricket ground with a scoreboard, a substantial pavilion and the truest wicket I ever batted on. It is no coincidence that the three best known cricketers it produced – Boycott, Moxon and Bird – were all opening bats. They learned on the perfect surface.

I joined the club 40 years ago. In those days you auditioned and waited for the call. The decision was sometimes one of life or death because the wickets we played on in the local leagues around Barnsley were death traps. We would have had a better chance of survival playing on the main line between Doncaster and Kings Cross.

My local club, where I grew up watching my father and later playing with him, was located in a farmer's backyard with cornfields on the boundary and daisies and buttercups in the outfield. The pavilion was made of wood and we had a huge tea pot, enamelled and bottomless.

Then we moved two fields away on to a brand new sports complex and for a while the pitch was a nightmare. Before the opening we instructed our groundsman, Old Cheyney, to produce a surface good enough to last for the official ceremony.

After that we would have to take our chance. His remedy was a strip concocted of marl and horse manure. "Oss muck. There's nowt like it," he'd say. He rolled it flat and let it set and although it looked an odd colour it certainly made a presentable batting surface.

On the day of the opening it rained and Cheyney's masterpiece became an evil smelling quagmire which necessitated the police evacuating people from their nearby homes. What is more, in receiving the ceremonial first ball to declare our new ground officially open, our captain played forward to a delivery of no great menace and lost his teeth.

This was not quite as dramatic as it sounds because the ball didn't hit him in the mouth but just below the heart. In fact, exactly on the breast pocket of his shirt which is where he stored his teeth while batting. Some time later we entertained the Barnsley second XI. This was important. This was us against the Folks Who Lived On The Hill. More importantly, this was my audition piece.

Our opening bowler at the time was a big lad called Terry Mac-Donald who was a pro boxer, and a good one. He was also quick and on our wicket unplayable and lethal. The Barnsley batsmen, coached to move into line with the head behind the ball, soon realised that such a technique would guarantee them a bed in the local infirmary.

They were chopped down but they didn't argue. For one thing Terry was too big but they also knew we had to play them on their patch. "Let us see how good you are on a proper wicket," is what they said.

I can remember to this day what it was like arriving at the ground. There was a man on the gate taking money. The scoreboard was like you saw at county grounds with an operator and individual as well as team scores so you needn't keep count in your head. I always did just in case the scorers missed a run. So did Geoffrey Boycott. But he auditioned later.

The dressing room had enough pegs for all of us and hot and cold running water. And when you walked down the steps in front of the

MICHAEL PARKINSON

pavilion you passed through a little gate on the way to the wicket. And what a wicket. Subsequently I played on all of Yorkshire's county grounds and later on most of our Test grounds and can honestly say that the wicket at Shaw Lane was as good as any. If you could play straight you could hang around for a long time with a walking stick. I did a lot of hanging around in the next few seasons. I wasn't much of a stroke player but I could certainly loiter.

This characteristic was noted during my audition performance by a man sitting by the sightscreen. Having observed me for about half an hour he shouted: "I don't know thi' name lad but I have to tell thi' tha's got about as much life as a bloody tombstone." I got to know him well over the coming season. He always sat in the same place and never changed his opinion of me.

As I walked to the wicket he would say in a loud voice: "Oh God, not 'im again." He was merciless but not particular. Anyone and everyone who played for Barnsley at that time suffered. He had a running feud with our skipper and pro, a nuggety little man called Ernie Steele. At that time the Barnsley Club, with commendable courage, had decided to blood young players in the first team. It was a brave decision because the Yorkshire League is one of the strongest and most competitive leagues in the land. It was also at a time when people used to watch league cricket, so we had our supporters to think of.

What it really meant was that Ernie Steele had a thankless task which he performed with great skill and forebearance. But there were times when the situation got the better of him. I remember playing once at Castleford, I think it was, against a young and fearsome quick bowler called Broughton who later played county cricket for Leicestershire.

I opened and didn't get too many in my half of the wicket from Mr Broughton, the majority of his deliveries bouncing way above my head. It wasn't that dangerous, but, on the other hand, it made scoring difficult. At the fall of a wicket Ernie Steele made his way to the middle carrying a pair of step ladders. It was a fair point to make but it wasn't very subtle. And it did much to improve Mr Broughton's aim.

During this period when we didn't win many games Ernie took some terrible stick from our regular barracker. I remember one match when we were getting a pasting in the field and every time the opposition hit a boundary our barracker would shout: "Put a man theer Ernie."

After this had been going on for some time Ernie lost his temper and rounding on his critic bellowed from the centre of the field: "And how many bloody fielders does tha' reckon I've got?" There was a pause and his critic shouted back: "Not bloody sufficient."

This wasn't the idyllic image of English club cricket. This wasn't about the smell of the cut grass and the gentle sound of leather on willow. This was altogether more rugged. This was the whiff of cordite and the sound of men at war.

The rules were simple. Show no mercy, expect none in return; take no prisoners. I was a battle scarred veteran aged 20 when I was joined at the wicket one afternoon by a 15-year-old wearing national health spectacles and a school cap. The fast bowler shouted to the stumper: "What's this then does tha' reckon?" "Looks like he's lost his mam," said the keeper.

All this by way of introducing the lad to the joys of playing with the men. The bowler winked at his colleague, marched back to the end of his run up quite convinced that this was a doddle. His first ball was just short and outside of the off stump whereupon he played the most beautiful back foot shot between the bowler and mid-off. It was classic in execution, the left elbow as high and pointed as a church steeple.

The ball whistled past the bowler and rattled the sightscreen. The bowler gave me a wry smile. "What's his name?" he asked. "Boycott. Geoffrey Boycott," I replied.

I don't even have to close my eye to see the young Boycott now, nor the unrazored Dickie Bird, nervous as a grasshopper, or the awesome Hubert Padgett, the best striker of a ball I ever saw at club level, or Graham Pearce, splayfooted, tireless, forever moaning but a marvellous bowler with the new ball. I remember fielding in the leg trap as Ellis Robinson bowled his off spin and watching in awe as George Barnett at cover point swooped and threw his flat whistling throw to the top of the stumps.

I remember the wind coming over the hill and the noise from Oakwell when the season overlapped. I remember learning the most beautiful of games in the best possible manner: on a decent wicket playing with men who knew.

If the time comes when there will no longer be a cricket pitch at Shaw Lane it will be a tragedy for the community and for Yorkshire cricket.

The Charity Commission says that the Shawlands Trust, which owns the ground, should get the best possible income for the charity. Is it not also the purpose of a local charity to be concerned about how best it can serve the people of the local community?

Anyone who has even the beginning of an idea about changing the use of the ground from anything other than a place where cricket is played should be aware that they are contemplating sacrilege. They should also know that the place is guarded by ghosts and that they are in danger of suffering the Curse of Parkinson.

They should tread softly. They are on hallowed ground.

Watching Chris Lewis gliding in to bowl or chasing and throwing in the outfield I started wondering if it would make sense for cricket to take a lesson from ice dancing and offer separate marks for style. Lewis would rate the maximum. One of the joys of cricket is that more than most other games, it not only allows its participants the opportunity for artistic expression, it also encourages it.

Moreover, it is the stylists who are framed in the mind's eye. One of the first times I visited Lord's was in 1946 to see Middlesex play Somerset and even though I was not yet at secondary school, I remember clearly a tall and immaculately attired opening batsman for Middlesex leaning on the ball and gently persuading it to all parts of the field. That was my first sight of J D Robertson. He scored a century and even now I can see one cover drive from the bowling of Arthur Wellard with the bat flowing in a full arc as if in slow motion and the ball speeding so quickly away that it hit the boundary before Robertson had completed his follow through.

The great K R Miller was the next stylist to make an impression on me. With Miller, it had as much to do with his broad shoulders, black wavy hair and natural swagger as his athleticism. No-one, except perhaps Viv Richards, ever walked onto a cricket field like Miller did. Miller looked as if he owned it, Richards as if he was about to fight for it.

I never missed a chance to watch Tom Graveney bat and was there ever a more graceful player than David Gower? Garfield Sobers wasn't half bad and thinking of West Indians there can have been few more fulfilling sights for the connoisseur than Frank Worrell with his eye in.

Of the Australians, I always loved to watch Greg Chappell bat. If you knew nothing of his background you would swear that he had learned the game at Eton and Fenners. The style was upright and classical in the tradition of the great post-war University batsmen like May, Cowdrey and Dexter.

And if we are awarding marks for bowling style, there are some fine arguments to be had. I never failed to be thrilled by Fred Trueman's run-up. I still think it the best action I ever saw because not only was it graceful and passionate, it was also as technically perfect in the delivery stride as a fast bowler can be.

Lillee, storming in with the crowd chanting was as awesome; Holding, rippling and silent like a curtain closing, was as menacing; Imran stretched and airborne at the moment of delivery, is as dramatic. But none, in my view, matched Fred. Rough-hewn he might have been, but there was a wonderful symmetry about his bowling.

I imagine it must have been a pleasure to have been bowled by Bishen Bedi. There was something almost deferential in his approach to the wicket. His enquiry to the umpire was courtly. To be bowled by Tony Lock was like being mugged. To be dismissed by Bedi was akin to being handed a letter by a man in a frock coat saying your services were no longer required.

I am, as you will by now be aware, on the way to picking my team of great stylists. I am missing a wicket-keeper. If a definition of style is making a difficult job look easy then Keith Andrew is my choice, if style is making a difficult job look impossible then Godfrey Evans would have few rivals. John Murray and Jeffrey Dujon were two wicket-keepers of great charm and elegance.

Here then is my All-Time XII for the World Style Cup:

J D Robertson, Barry Richards, Tom Graveney, David Gower, Greg Chappell, Garfield Sobers, Keith Andrew, Dennis Lillee, Michael Holding, F S Trueman, Bishen Bedi, K R Miller.

I am sure there are great stylists I have overlooked.

There are, of course, no absolute judgements to be made about style. Except to say that it is much easier to detect than to acquire.

David Gower has been much in my thoughts this week. I was thinking about favourite grounds and remembering that the last time I saw him play in a Test match was at Sydney when he scored a century of effortless charm. Later that week he turned out in a charity beach cricket match and, watching him play, I realised he is the only man I have ever seen who plays exactly the same way on a beach as he does in a Test match.

I was having these memories sitting under the hedge at Bray thinking that if there was a more beautiful ground in all the world than the one I was looking at then I should be very surprised. I did play on one which came near, however. It was when I was doing my National Service and stationed in Wiltshire. One Sunday we travelled deep into the countryside to find a local village ground. It was called Combe Wallop or Middle Wallop or some such. We came upon it at the back of a thatched pub in a fold in the hills. There was a smell of cut grass and wood smoke. A donkey pulled the roller.

The opponents were large men, farmers, ruddy of face, cautious by nature. Their umpire wore a floppy hat with fishing flies stuck in it. The sun shone, birds sang and there was nowhere in the world I would rather have been. What is more I had a new Gunn and Moore I wanted to try out and this seemed the ideal opportunity.

Their opening bowler lolloped in, I played well forward and was hit on the pad outside the off-stump. The bowler appealed and the umpire stuck his finger up. I couldn't believe it. I stayed in position stretched down the track, leg outside the line.

"That's not out, Mr Umpire," I said. He took another look as if reconsidering his decision. Then he said: "Might not be out where you come from, but down here it is." So much for Paradise.

It is difficult for people who don't know about cricket to understand how much of its appeal derives from its setting. Before coming to Bray I played at Datchet, another charming ground. I was working in America for the BBC when I was invited to spend a weekend with

Hugh Hefner at his Playboy mansion. I told Mr Hefner's assistant that I would not be able to take up his kind invitation. She seemed shocked. People did not turn down a chance to romp with Hef and the Bunnies.

"What should I tell Mr Hefner?" she asked. Tell him the truth, I thought. "Say to him that I can't join him at the weekend because I'm playing cricket at Datchet," I said. There was a long silence at the end of the 'phone and then a click as the receiver was replaced. I never heard from Mr Hefner again, nor did he come to Datchet to see the opposition. Had he done so he would have been even more confused.

In those days I used to play. Now I just watch. Our other spectator turned up at the weekend. Every season he brings his chair down and sits between the sightscreen and the pavilion. He is equipped for all eventualities. He has a parasol and a golf visor for the sun, an umbrella and a plastic cocoon for the rain and a balaclava, ear muffs and a bottomless thermos for when the temperature falls below freezing. He also carries a large anchor to stop him being blown away when the winds sweep in from the west.

He rarely misses a game and when he does we send someone round to his house to see that he's all right. The only spectator to have seen more cricket is the church in the corner. It has been there 700 years next year and we're having a special game to celebrate the occasion. If we invited all the players who have been to our ground in recent years there would be a team and a half.

They still talk of Graeme Pollock playing at Bray and straight driving the ball over the sightscreen and across the road on to the village green. I didn't see that, but I did see Intikhab Alam hit the biggest drive made on the ground. He flat-batted one of our bowlers back over his head, over the net which was supposed to stop balls being hit out of the ground, over the houses and into the middle of the Thames where it hit a passing pleasure boat.

It was on this ground that Tom Graveney batted a couple of years ago. A young quickie fancied his chances and fired one in short. Tom deftly flicked him into the churchyard for six. I have seen Barry Richards bat at Bray and Geoffrey Boycott and Gordon Greenidge. I have seen Dennis Lillee run in from the river end and Imran Khan, too. There will be more to come this season, Yorkshire make an annual visit.

Will young Tendulkar join the list of those who have played in the

most beautiful of settings?

All this I was thinking the other day, sitting under a hedge looking at a beautiful ground, sniffing a new season. I was thinking that when Goochie has done with him, David Gower might join us at Bray and play out his career in surroundings appropriate to his matchless style.

Whenever I stare out across our ground or think of David Gower I know why I love the game as I do.

I am at the age when I have to consider whether or not the next game of cricket I play will be my last. When I have finished writing this article I take myself to Chippinghurst Manor in Oxfordshire where Victor Blank hosts an annual match between business tycoons like Richard Branson, cricket legends like Sir Garfield Sobers and odds and sods like me and David Frost. Mr Frost is skippering my side. I see he has me at number nine, signifying I am being played for my bowling which nowadays is on the slow side of brisk. By this I mean I manage to bustle to the wicket looking like I mean business but because of rust in the delivery stride the ball takes longer to reach the batsman than I intended. I am nowhere near as slow as Mr Tim Rice, the speed of whose deliveries can be measured on a sun dial and who has been known to pursue his career as a songwriter in the time available between the ball leaving his hand and reaching the batsman. The difference is, of course, that Mr Rice bowls that way out of choice whereas I have no say in the matter. Nowadays my style is the result of wear and tear. If this is to be my last game of cricket then there could be few more pleasant spots to end a career. The ground sits in a fold in the hills, on the doorstep of a lovely manor house surrounded by trees, a stream and pasture land. It is as different as can be imagined from where I played my very first game of proper cricket which had a splendid view of Grimethorpe Colliery at one end and a farmyard at the other. I was eleven when they first let me play with my heroes and I remember them clearly more than forty years on.

There were our two big hitters, Mr Roberts and Mr Stewardson. George Roberts had one leg and an eye like a sparrow hawk, Norman Stewardson was built like a pit bull terrier and had a bat bound in a mysterious brown skin which he swore was kangaroo hide. Whatever it was it enabled him to smite the ball immense distances. Then there was Jack Berry, our all rounder, one of the best bowlers I ever saw in league cricket. He bowled medium pace leg breaks in the manner of D. V. P. Wright with a googly thrown in just to keep the batsmen

honest. I doubt if many of the batsmen he baffled in our division of
the Barnsley and District League were capable of spotting his googly.
The great majority were probably unaware that such a ball existed.
They were too busy trying to hit him into the next parish, and failing.
Our wicketkeeper was Minty Rowe who kept in flat cap and brass
buckled belt. His protector was made of metal and made a noise like a
gong when struck by the ball. He stood up to everyone, including our
fast bowler, Mr Baker who took a run so long that we had to cut a
hole in the hedge at one end of the ground. Our other opening
bowler was my dear father who modelled his action on his great hero
Harold Larwood. I can see him now, slim as a whip, wavy hair flop-
ping, gliding in, rearing a bouncer past the batsman's defence. He
loved bowling bouncers and then having a chat with the batsman.
Nothing offensive. He talked to everyone on the cricket field:
umpires, spectators, opponents. The only time he was quiet was when
he was running in to bowl. No one loved the game of cricket more
than he, and no one gained more joy from it.

There was a big brown tea pot in our pavilion and a lady in a pinny
making potted meat sandwiches. When we batted I had to score and I
would climb a ladder into the loft which was cool and still and the
perfect place to daydream about playing for England. In this regard, at
least, I started with a better facility than I ended with because the
changing facilities at Mr Blank's ground are a brace of wigwams.
Looking down my team I see that I am in good company. The list
reads: Dennis Amiss (Warwickshire and England), Sunil Gavaskar
(India), Clive Lloyd (Lancashire and West Indies), Imran Khan (Pakistan), Mike Brearley (Middlesex and England), Phil Edmonds (Middlesex and England), John Snow (Sussex and England), David Frost
(TV AM and England) and M. Parkinson (Barnsley and England). I
am delighted that Mr Edmonds is on my side. The last time I played
he was in the opposing team and bowling when I went to the wicket.
As I took guard I imagined I would be given one off the mark, it
being a jovial game for charity and Mr Edmonds and his charming
wife both being friends of mine. His first ball turned, bounced and hit
me on the forearm whereupon Mr Edmonds appealed for lbw and
brought up two short legs. I managed to survive the over and
approached Mr Edmonds for clarification of the situation. He
explained that he couldn't play cricket any way other than seriously
and that when he saw me coming to the wicket he didn't see a friend

but an easy victim for the career record. I hear that the latest casualty of Mr Edmonds' enthusiasm is the well-known actor Mr Peter O'Toole who turned out recently hoping for an hour or so at the crease only to be caught first ball by Mr Edmonds diving many yards to his left and holding a screamer inches from the turf. When I pointed out this was no way to treat Lawrence of Arabia Mr Edmonds said that in his view the man who wrote *The Seven Pillars of Wisdom* must take his chance at the crease like the rest of the human race.

I always thought that Phil Edmonds ought to have been born in Sheffield. He would have made a perfect Yorkshireman. He and Brian Close are blood brothers. Mr Close is missing this year which is sad because we shall be denied the incisive comments about the state of play from a man whose passion for the game is a bottomless well. A couple of years ago, with Imran Khan in full spate, Brian persuaded our skipper that he had worked out the way to dismiss the captain of Pakistan. Whereupon Imran smote four straight sixes and two majestic fours from the over, each shot as graceful as it was powerful. I walked alongside Brian as he trudged away. "Nivver could bowl to a bloody slogger like him," he said. In the same game, Martin Crowe, fielding under a large sun hat in the deep, took two of the most spectacular catches you will ever see. After the second I was approached by Mike Brearley. "Wonderful fielder for a businessman," he said, mistaking the captain of New Zealand for a city tycoon. Both incidents made me wonder: were they like that when they captain England or was it the job that did for them?

My great worry this year has been finding the gear to play in. Every year it gets more difficult. With three sons who play cricket it was never easy. I once went to find my kit only to discover that the bat was being used by Number One Son at Ickenham, my trousers were on a field in some distant part of Buckinghamshire and my cock box was doing duty at Uxbridge. I am now reduced to borrowing their kit. Andrew has legs like a giraffe so his trousers finish under my chin. His gloves are Duncan Fearnley 405s and bear as much resemblance to the Sugg's wraparound sausages that I began my career with as a space suit to a fig leaf.

I am glad to see the bat is a Gunn and Moore, but this is a bludgeon compared to the wand of my youth. Are young men stronger nowadays? They must have larger hands because I cannot get my fingers round the bat handle it is so thick with rubbers. To sum

up: wrongly attired, discomfited, stiff of limb, unsound of wind, bereft of sporting ambition, hoping to survive without breaking a limb is how I shall take the field in a few hours' time. For the last time? I think so. But all it will take to bring me back next year is one that turns enough to beat the bat, or a sweet four through the covers or a catch that sticks and reminds me of what used to be. It is when the sun shines on an English cricket ground and you hear the birdsong and smell the cut grass that you think most longingly about the possibility of immortality.

John Arlott said: "Meet me at the Grace Gates and we will watch Middlesex play your lot and drink a decent claret." And we did. Fred bowled fast which always made John thirsty. I think we had a gentle kip in the afternoon and later in the bar I said it had been a perfect day and wasn't I the luckiest man in the world because I was paid to watch cricket and interview Rita Hayworth.

John thought a bit about this and then said he thought he had the better job because *The Guardian* paid him to watch cricket and drink wine. He told me he once had a similar conversation with Neville Cardus who said: "But my dear John, I am a much more fortunate fellow than you." John asked how that could be. "Because" said Neville, "*The Guardian* pay me to watch the cricket and go to the opera and upon mature reflection I would rather sleep with a soprano than a wine merchant."

That was before the melancholy set in with John. It was upsetting for his many friends that later in his life he seemed remote from the genuine love and respect they had to offer. His was a unique contribution to a game and for all he gave cricket poetic imagery and romance, he remained clear that it was only a game.

He maybe would have wished for a career in politics, something more substantial perhaps than commentating on cricket. Yet, as he once told me: "Politics govern everything we do, the games we play, the way we play them, who we play. Politics controls life because politics is the philosophy by which you live, exist and behave."

That being the case, John Arlott influenced more people than most, not just about a game, but about the eternal verities of beauty, companionship and, above all, humour. He didn't just commentate on cricket, he told us an awful lot about ourselves.

I have never been able to work out why people want to watch darts being played on television. Train spotting would be more interesting, a visit to a caravan site much more riveting.

And yet there was a time, not too long ago, when the bibulous features of Jocky Wilson were promoted as belonging to an athlete of note and many were promoting the claims of Eric Bristow, the Crafty Cockney, as our Sportsman of the Year.

The elevation of a pleasant pub pastime to an international sport worthy of 100 hours of television coverage a year is what happens when you get television executives who don't mind what they sell and viewers who don't care what they buy.

Nowadays ITV don't cover the sport at all and BBC devote 22 hours to darts, which only goes to prove that in the recent shake-up of ITV the Government had the right idea but chose the wrong organisation.

Watching the final stages of the World Darts Championship this weekend I was struck by the discrepancy between the tumult at the event and my own steady breathing and regular pulse.

Dear old Sid Waddell did his best to stoke things up. According to Sid, I was watching "brutal darts", there was one player who needed "plastic surgery to his ego" and supporters of a player from Merseyside were "biting their teeth". Sadly there were no pictures to match any of Sid's commentary.

For all his enthusiasm and genuine passion there was no disguising the fact that what I was seeing was ordinary repetitious and ultimately boring.

In an attempt to liven things up and freshen media interest the game has done much to smarten up its act. The players' clothes are an improvement on what went before, though the shirts still belong to that variety normally seen on our beaches.

The sad fact is that the more they try to design a different image for darts the more they expose the frailty of the product.

The wisest statement ever made about the game was that you can take darts out of the pub but you can't take the pub out of darts. It belongs in the world of beer bellies, belches, baggy shirts, bleary eyes and booze. It doesn't survive the arc-light scrutiny of television, not without changing character, and when it does that it loses its soul.

Mind you, it should be pointed out that although we are talking about the game in crisis, Phil Taylor, who won the title of world champion on Saturday night, collected a cheque for £28,000. This is considerably more than county cricketers make for playing an entire season.

Also, I can think of several internationals in what I would describe as more legitimate sports who might wish they were afflicted by the sort of crisis the darts is at present suffering.

It does seem absurd that two men throwing darts at a board share between them more than £40,000 for an evening's work which is more than Derek Randall ever earned for a full season's work as an international cricketer.

I was thinking as I was writing about Derek and re-living the memories: who could write an article, never mind a book, about the Great Moments of Darts? When was the time that the feats of Jocky Wilson stirred the imagination and made strong men misty-eyed? Who will wax lyrical about Phil Taylor?

Darts is a prime example of our capacity to celebrate the mediocre in sport. Frank Bruno is another, so are most of our football teams.

Sadly, little will change until television adopts a more critical attitude. It is one thing to promote a sport, it is quite another to hoodwink the public.

There are signs that the customers are smarter than the television executives give them credit for, hence the decline of darts. But it won't be a credible situation until darts are taken totally from our screens, along with Frank Bruno and other pugilists concocted by television.

Bruno is not as "thick as two short planks". But when he stands in the ring and looks around him he could claim to know a lot of people who are.

When they ask me in the future what it was like at Twickenham when we beat France in '91, I'll say it was so tense that, when Hodgkinson converted Underwood's try, the only sound to be heard was the swish of his leg on the down swing.

Similarly, when pressed for details of the first French try, I will say it had more to do with sorcery than sport. After all, what proof do any of us have that the ball Blanco collected under his own posts was the one Saint-André crossed the England line with at the other end of the field?

It was a sullen day for a triumph, but somehow the perfect setting. The England side in their present mood are not made for sunshine and fancy weather. They were designed to grapple in mud, to bow heads against the wind and rain, and plough their way through life rather than gallivant across sun-dappled meadows. What made it such a fascinating contest was the contrast between the fanciful French and the obdurate English.

There were times – specifically the three French tries – when one might have been tempted to list the qualities of both sides:

FRENCH	ENGLISH
Wind	Earth
Blaze	Smoulder
Colourful	Monochrome
Imaginative	Pragmatic
Devil may care	Dogged
Plumed cavalry	Shire horse
Maigret	PC Plod

Yet there was no doubt at the end that France had been well and deservedly beaten by the better team. In the final analysis, the old cliché about only playing as well as your opponents allow you to come up freshly minted and, while it is undeniably true that one or two of the French players contributed hugely towards the downfall of their team, it is also a fact that it helps to have nerves of steel and no

imagination whatsoever when facing up to the English forwards.

Those who carp at England's style and say the team are boring will have learned from this match that England have far more options for the future than the French. The foundations of England's organisation are so well structured that anything is possible. If, and when, improvisation comes, it will be based on a sound technique. The French on the other hand will remain colourful mavericks so long as they rely on a mixture of their own imagination and divine intervention to get them out of trouble.

The crowd at Twickenham knew the truth of it. Their team had given them what they wanted, namely victory over the French and the Grand Slam and it didn't matter that they didn't come served on a silver salver with all the trimmings. Twickenham spectators are a friendly mob to be among, knowledgeable, fair minded and, so far as I could tell, not given to spitting, skull-splitting and knee-capping their neighbours, or other anti-social pastimes indulged by spectators at some events I could mention. As with the rugby league final (will I be banned from Twickers forever?) there is the comforting feeling of being safe in a big crowd and part of a pleasant occasion. If only . . .

In the crowd leaving the ground there was much talk about England winning the World Cup. They could be forgiven their optimism. It had been, in more ways than one, a intoxicating day. What we had witnessed we would all talk about and embroider upon in years to come.

It might have been the occasion or it might have been something I drank, but as I waited for my transport and looked back at the stadium, I imagined it taking off with music playing and lights flashing rather like the spaceship in *Close Encounters*. It would have been the perfect finale.

As it was, it remained windswept and sodden and firmly rooted in the clay that shaped it. A bit like the England team, come to think of it.

More often than not it's where we are born that dictates our sporting lives. A short bus trip was all that stood between me and a lifetime addiction to rugby league. In those days the game started just below Wakefield and ended just above Leeds and the rest was soccer. Barnsley was soccer, but now and again when the lads were away in some remote place like Birmingham, we would go to Wakefield to see the Trinity.

There were giants in those days like Lewis Jones, Billy Boston and Brian Bevan who ran at an opponent while looking at the turf and sidestepped off both feet like a Jack rabbit. They were the stuff of legends.

The fact is it took a long time for me to be wooed away from soccer, but it has happened. I am now convinced that rugby league is our finest winter sport. It might have happened quicker had my introduction to the game as a player been less traumatic. This occurred during my last year at school when a group of missionaries from Wakefield came among us bearing an oval ball.

It is at this point in the story that I must introduce you to Poxon. He was a large, strong and ugly youth whose adenoids caused him to walk around with a permanently open and leaking mouth. Added to constantly watery eyes Poxon always looked as if he had just been saved from drowning.

When I look back upon my education, such as it was, I realise that I spent 75 per cent of my time devising means of keeping out of Poxon's way. An encounter could prove fatal. At playtime he would stand near the toilets, picking his nose, scanning the playground for someone to terrorise. As an athlete he was good at anything which involved him being battered about the head. Thus he excelled at boxing and made a fine stopper centre-half where he gave the game a new dimension by using his head to tackle an opponent.

His most original technique he saved for the high jump. He invented what can only be termed the Poxon Dive, running straight at the

bar and hurling himself over at full speed. Sometimes he would remember to break the fall with his hands. More often than not he wouldn't bother and his head would leave a large hole in the sand pit.

When the disciples of rugby league arrived at our school they saw Poxon and fell upon him. He was large, uncomplicated, impervious to pain – either his own or someone else's. They made him captain of the Possibles. I was on the other side and positioned at full-back. We played on a pitch with a dramatic slope in the middle. It was such that if you stood under the posts at one end you couldn't see the posts at the other.

I was staring into infinity, thinking about Alice Faye and Vera Hruba Ralston when I heard a rumbling noise and felt the ground tremble. I looked towards the far horizon. It was empty. Then, just like in a John Ford movie, the ridge was filled with whooping savages. At the front was Poxon, head back, mouth open, water from his eyes and nose streaming behind him like vapour trails.

He was heading in my direction and he was going to mullycrush me. It was then I decided that rugby played no part in my future and that, indeed, if I was to have a future, I had better move. I did, I turned and ran. I was halfway to the changing rooms when I suddenly realised that Poxon was still pursuing me. What they hadn't told him was that it was not necessary to kill the full-back to get maximum points.

I locked myself in the toilets, which is where the Wakefield missionaries found Poxon just before he started to demolish the door with his head. I was in deep shock for days and it was many years before I could even hear mention of the word rugby without breaking into a sweat.

So how did it come to pass that I became convinced of the game's virtues and now prefer it to soccer? I suppose Eddie Waring was an early influence. I know he was a controversial character in the sense that rugby purists found it hard to stomach his hearty, often slapstick style. But the fact is no-one has played a more significant part in spreading the game's popularity, nor has any commentator so effortlessly captured the pawky humour of the average spectator.

My favourite Waring commentary occurred when the camera dwelt for an embarrassingly long time upon a player who had been whacked in what cricket commentators define as "the box". The victim was in agony, head bowed when Eddie Waring explained everything with the immortal line: "I want you to know, ladies and gentleman, that whatever else he might be doing yon fella is not praying."

He was the voice of the terraces. It could have been him, but wasn't, who was near me at a Wembley final when a prissy and diminutive referee attempted to have a word in the ear of a huge forward. As he beckoned the player down to his level my neighbour said: "Ayup ref, why doesn't tha' stand on thi' 'andbag?"

The simple fact is that going to a rugby match nowadays is to be reminded of what it was like going to soccer before the yobs took over, both on and off the field. Why is it you can move among 90,000 people at Wembley for a rugby league final and be part of a happy throng, yet would be foolish even to contemplate doing the same at an FA Cup final unless you were given covering fire by a helicopter gun ship?

These are people from the same part of Britain. From Lancashire and Yorkshire, from the same socio-economic groups. So what accounts for the difference? I wouldn't dare to attempt an answer except to suggest that perhaps there is something about the spirit of rugby that commands respect.

Perhaps the sight of players uncomplainingly accepting the referee's ruling might find a response in the crowd. Perhaps it has been more skilfully administered by its executive than soccer has. It could hardly be worse.

Perhaps if rugby league develops to the point where it becomes a truly potent competitor to soccer – and it deserves to – it might have the effect of convincing the people who run that sport of the need for radical change. I doubt it, but no matter. Next Saturday, in the deciding Test between Britain and Australia, we know we will see a game of commitment and skill, of courage and finesse.

We know that when we see Ellery Hanley we are watching one of the world's great athletes, that Martin Offiah in full flight is one of the supreme spectacles in any sport and that Mal Meninga's dignity and composure redefines style as being grace under pressure. We also know that the referee will stand no nonsense and that the terraces will provide a chorus appropriate to the event without the need to resort to the four-letter words and racial abuse that are so much a part of the other game.

The fact is, as I read what I have written, I now know what happened. I didn't leave soccer. The truth is it gave me up.

Wembley Stadium was a good place to be on Saturday if you like watching great teams in action. What we witnessed in Wigan beating Castleford was not simply the best team in rugby league winning yet another trophy, but the best club side in all of professional sport.

If the definition of a great team involves a unique blend of invincibility and glamour, a combination of organisation and imagination, then it is difficult to imagine another outfit so completely qualified as Wigan.

At club level in soccer we have to think back to the golden days of Best, Charlton and Law; in cricket the Surrey side of the Fifties under Surridge would make the grade, as would the Yorkshire team when Close, Illingworth and Trueman were running things.

But none of them, great as they were, so completely dominated their game as Wigan do. There is an inexorable quality about the club's progress to Wembley and the winning of the trophy that, at the present time, cannot be denied.

On Saturday not all the limitless and seemingly inexhaustible guts and energy of the Castleford players, not the relentless support of their fans, not all the prayers being offered from Yorkshire and the uncommitted areas that Wigan might come unstuck, made the slightest bit of difference.

A request for divine inspiration is not enough. What is required against this Wigan side is nothing short of divine intervention.

Having said all that, it must also be stated that this was not one of Wigan's greatest performances. This was nothing like the semi-final thrashing of Bradford Northern by 71 points to 10 which was as ruthless in its unflagging determination as it was breathtaking in the sublime manner of its execution. In years to come old men will drink many a free pint bought to loosen their tongues and tell what they saw on that day.

Castleford are cast in different metal to Bradford Northern.

Whereas Bradford stood back and admired Wigan's handiwork, the Castleford players got stuck in. There was something heroic about their commitment but it was never going to be enough. This Wigan team can play any game the opposition chooses and, when their opponents have run out of ideas, can come up with one or two notions of their own.

They fashion their own rhythms and tempos within a game. It is like watching a great boxer at work. There are times when Wigan put their backs to the ropes and bob and weave. Then, unexpectedly and often in devastating fashion, there comes the counter-attack. Sometimes they maul the opposition, coming in toe to toe, slugging it out.

Best of all is when they surge forwards in unrelenting attack, flickering the ball between them across the line, testing every inch of the opposition's defence. At those moments the fulcrum of the team is one of the unlikeliest looking athletes in all of sport. Andy Gregory seems to have been assembled from several different sources. For one thing he is only five-and-a-half feet tall yet his legs are six feet long. How can this be? Part of the illusion is due to Mr Gregory's shorts which would be indecent on anyone more glamorous than he.

As it is, they fit so tightly about his crotch that I fear his substitution on Saturday could have been as much due to self-inflicted circulatory problems as any damage the opposition might have caused him. This is not to say Mr Gregory is a figure of fun. Far from it. He might look a rum 'un but he is one of the greatest playmakers ever to step on to a rugby field.

Martin Offiah, on the other hand, looks like what he is. Even in repose he resembles a coiled spring. In full flight he challenges the spectator to adequately describe what he sees. He doesn't run – not in the accepted sense like you and me – he doesn't bolt, career, dart, gallop, scamper, scurry, speed or leg it. What he does is more exciting and graceful than that. We will have to invent a new verb: to offiah, which means to achieve maximum acceleration with the minimum of fuss and optimum style.

He 'offiahed' past Graeme Bradley in the second half, side-stepping him with such precision and pace that the player was spun around like a man trapped in a revolving door. When he scored his first try he went through a defender's bodycheck as if bursting through a paper hoop and when he scored his second try you knew that what you had just seen was one of the world's most remarkable athletes in action.

It is almost a cliché to observe that Wembley was a pleasant place to be for the rugby league cup final; that not for the first time, walking away from the ground, mingling happily with fans from both teams, I was reminded that soccer used to be like this before the yobbos took over.

Why should rugby league be so different? Well, both the Prime Minister and Mr David Mellor were at Wembley on Saturday. What they saw, both as sports lovers and politicians, will have given them much to think about.

As we drove away from Wembley news was coming through of riot police presiding over the last rites of another football season. Next season troublemakers will be required to be seated before they riot and, given the hike in prices at some grounds, will have to pay more for the privilege of a punch-up.

The saddest news of all is that Fulham have probably played their last game at Craven Cottage. Oakwell apart (Oakwell is the home of Barnsley FC), I felt that the Cottage was my spiritual home. The people on the terraces were the same long suffering, philosophical souls I stood among at Barnsley. On the field of play the same collection of magicians and misfits. This collaboration was celebrated most notably at Fulham in the relationship between Johnny Haynes and Tosh Chamberlain.

Now if you never saw them play all you would need to know was that Haynes was one of the greatest players we have ever produced and Chamberlain wasn't. More than that Haynes was perfectionist, a man who measured his passes in millimetres, whose brain worked with the sophistication and cunning of a chess master.

Chamberlain was a pixilated fellow, a creature of whimsical manner, a chap much influenced by the shifting of the tides and the movement of the planet through space. Together they were Mutt and Jeff, Laurel and Hardy, Old Mother Riley and her daughter Kitty. The good Lord created Haynes to go to Craven Cottage and be reminded of his own mortality by the presence of Chamberlain. He simply told Chamberlain: "Tosh, old son, you go out there and get bollocked by Haynsey."

And this is what happened and why Craven Cottage was a happy, smiling place to be during those years. The classic image of those days is Haynes standing hands on hips enquiring of Chamberlain why his inch-perfect through ball had ended up on a passing coal barge in the

River Thames and Tosh explaining about the wind and the divots and his boot lace coming undone.

Sometimes Tosh fought back, indeed, he was once booked by the ref for having a row with Haynes on the field. "You can't do that ref, he's on my side," said Tosh. But it didn't matter. They were golden days.

One year, when Fulham were in danger of relegation, a few of us hired a band and a boat and cruised up river to see the last game of the season. We moored by the ground and a musician played the last post. A fan behind the goals threw a brick and broke his trumpet. So much for laments.

The last time I went to see Fulham play George Best and Rodney Marsh were clowning and scheming on the park. It was a proper setting for two great entertainers. They are ghosts now from Fulham's past along with Macedo, Langley, Eddie Lowe, Graham Leggatt, Maurice Cook, Jimmy Hill, Haynes, Tosh and the rest. They are memories of a past when the game was fun to watch and play.

There aren't enough people to want to watch Fulham nowadays and it's not Fulham but the game that is to blame. The Premier League is not a bright future for soccer built on the base of a new structure. What it looks like is the same mess under different management. Even the players are not convinced. Lineker's away, so reportedly are Barnes and Walker. Gascoigne has opted out. Where are the premier players for the Premier League?

The only good thing to come from the entire carve-up is that Barnsley are finally in the First Division. I knew it would happen one day, I just didn't know how.

There is not much to be said about that heavyweight fight last week except that it made you nostalgic for the likes of Brian London, Richard Dunn and dear old Joe Bugner. All it proved was that Gary Mason has the mobility of a lamp post and Lennox Lewis is a nice name.

The commentary by Frank Bruno was what it deserved and we can only hope that the speculation on whether or not Harry's mate fights the winner was, like the rest of the evening, not to be taken seriously. What made a mediocre event even more second-rate by comparison was the BBC's decision to show a television recording of the first fight between Joe Frazier and Mohammed Ali. With, I am sure, unconscious humour, the producers of the Lewis-Mason fight decided it should be held on the 20th anniversary of one of the great heavyweight contests of all time.

It could be argued that the decision was justified in that, roughly speaking, Lewis and Mason were doing the same job as Ali and Frazier, but this only works if you believe that a clog dancer and Fred Astaire are peas from the same pod. For me, the film was a reminder that whenever fight fans gather to discuss the three great contests between Ali and Frazier, no-one ever mentions the part I played in Smokin' Joe's preparation, and eventual downfall.

What is not generally known is that for a while, I was Joe Frazier's sparring partner. My career lasted three rounds and I retired from the job after taking a left hook to the head which loosened several screws.

What exactly happened I shall tell you later, but first let me recount how I came to be Joe's punchbag. The story started that day 20 years ago when the two met at Madison Square Garden in what was, indisputably, the greatest heavyweight contest I have ever witnessed. There wasn't a phoney moment in it. Even the hype was real.

It wasn't, of course, the holy war; nor was it GI Joe against the draft-dodger. But it was a fight to the finish between two great athletes who had a genuine dislike of each other. The politically committed, quick-witted Ali saw in the quieter, more self-effacing Frazier the complaisant, uncomplaining black. He called him 'Uncle Tom.'

Frazier's resentment was based not so much on the crudity of the remark as the cruelty of the lie. He once said: "I'm a *black* man. I'm blacker than him. He's got a nice *brown* body."

He knew also what poverty meant; he picked vegetables for a dollar a day, was one of nine children.

Ali, by comparison, had a comfortable upbringing. He never had to work, except at being a prizefighter. He grew up with the kind of physique and looks that other men envy. An American sportswriter once said he would love to borrow Mohammed Ali's body for 48 hours as there were "three guys I'd like to beat up and four women I'd like to make love to."

Had Mohammed Ali been an actor, he would have been given the Sidney Poitier part in Guess Who's Coming To Dinner. But if the director had wanted Joe Frazier, the film would never have been made. Frazier summed it all up when Ali said: "I am going to give him a ghetto whuppin." "What does he know about a ghetto whipping?" said Smokin' Joe.

So we knew before the fight that this was the genuine article. This was the fight that couldn't be fixed; whatever the outcome, it would be properly arrived at. Whenever I remember that night, I first see the beautiful spectators in exotic furs, wide-brimmed, plumed hats, high-heeled boots. And they were the men.

And then I remember it was the night I knew I didn't have to justify my reason for being there, to be concerned about sitting at ringside watching two men trying to knock each other senseless. The fact is that Ali and Frazier were made in heaven and sent out upon the land to fight one another. In boxing terms, they were the perfect match.

Frazier was the slugger; hooking and uppercutting from a crouch. Ali was the artist; feinting, swaying, improvising. Frazier was remorseless; forever moving forward, taking two punches to get one in.

Ali boxed like a creature of mood; a languid, even listless phase suddenly culminating in a blaze of energy with punches as swift and spectacular as forked lightning. It was, simply, unforgettable.

What it meant to me was not simply a desire to be at the next fight between the two men, but to try to somehow capture on television the build-up to the encounter. Which is how I came to be Joe Frazier's sparring partner.

We devised a television co-production with myself and an American interviewer plus Ali and Frazier in a New York Studio on the eve of their second fight. It was decided I should spend a few days filming Joe Frazier so that we could show him in training as an introduction to the programme.

I don't know who suggested that I should get in the ring with Smokin' Joe. I didn't volunteer. In the couple of days I had spent in his company, I had grown to like Frazier a lot. He was so charming and polite that he didn't even laugh when we stripped and changed in the same dressing room. All that can be said about a comparison between our two physiques is that not only was God very clever but He also had a wonderful sense of humour.

Nor did I compare well when dressed for the encounter. The borrowed shorts had obviously belonged to a Sumo wrestler. My arms, which have always been on the thin side, looking even more puny with boxing gloves the size of pillow cases attached to the ends.

As I clambered into the ring, I felt the curiosity of the audience turn to hate. These were true boxing aficionados, men who frequent gymnasiums and watch boxers work out, men with knowing faces.

They gave me a glance, shook their heads and no doubt thought the champ was soft in the head to get mixed up in a publicity stunt with a limey famine victim. When we shook hands, it suddenly struck me that Frazier's arms were the size of my legs and his neck was nearly as far round as my chest.

Beforehand, in the dressing room, the former heavyweight champion of the world had asked me about my previous experience. I told him I had fought Sonny Shaw in the playground at the Snydale Road Infants' School, Cudworth, and a Lance Corporal Smithers in an army barracks at Devizes, Frazier said he didn't know either fighter, but all I had to do for the purpose of our encounter was to keep on jabbing whereupon he would move inside, pretend to throw a few punches, and whisper the next move in my ear.

He was as good as his word, and better. He would slip inside my tentative left arm, hammer away at my body as if he meant it, but all the time just pulling the punch an inch from the point of contact. Then he would spin me round like a dancing partner, whisper 'left hook, right hook' and move away.

Soon my fear deserted me. Soon, I began to believe it was Smokin' Joe versus Punchin' Parky. It was a dangerous illusion. Joe was

149

choreographing the third and final round and making it look believable when I decided to change the script.

I cannot recall precise details for reasons which will become obvious, but at any event as Joe came in, slipping my lead, I swung a right which hit him on the side of the head. As I did it I realised my mistake. After all, I had struck a man who had been the heavyweight champion of the world, a man who could rip my head off if he so desired. Frazier shook his head in mock confusion, gave me a knowing smile and then hit me with a left hook.

By his definition it was a tap to the head, a gentle reminder not to be silly. The problem is that fit and strong men like Joe Frazier have little idea of their own strength in relation to the rest of the human race. He felt he had gently chastised me; I felt as if I had walked into a wardrobe. The legs went at the knees and I heard bells. Frazier settled matters by raising my hand and walking me round the ring as the victor. In fact he was holding me up.

The spectators kept their eyes firmly on the racing pages and I slumped on a bench where I was left to contemplate my foolishness as Frazier went to work on the heavy bag. Eddie Futch, his trainer, worked him harder than usual whipping him to a controlled frenzy by telling him he was punching like a girl, taunting him with the latest Ali prediction until the heavy bag, with the trainer clinging to it, was being moved from side to side and backwards and forwards by the ferocity of the blows.

When Futch wrapped it up with "OK champ, that's enough for the day," Frazier turned from the bag, sweat pouring from him, eyes glinting with anger. He was looking for something to hit. He drove his fist into the pine strip wall of the gymnasium with such power that an air conditioning unit above his head jumped from its seating.

A few days later, we sat together in a television studio while Mohammed Ali took over the show, as he always did when given an even chance.

It was one of Ali's more extraordinary performances. He wasn't selling tickets. He didn't need to. He was involving us all in his fantasies, demonstrating the full range of his remarkable personality. One moment he would be braying at the moon, the next he would be sensibly reflecting upon the reasons why he chose not to be drafted in the American army.

In the commercial breaks he would taunt Joe Frazier to the limit, calling him 'dumb,' asking how he thought he had the right to share a stage with one so clever and pretty. During one break he stood before Frazier punctuating his insults by snapping his fingers under his opponent's nose.

He timed it perfectly so that at the moment Frazier rose from his seat, excited and angry to confront his tormentor, we were back on air and Ali was revealed having a joke with the hosts while Frazier, for no reason the viewers could discern, was on his feet looking grim and menacing.

The fight was something of an anti-climax. It was bound to be so when compared to the first encounter. Frazier lost, but only just and Ali went on to regain the title and dream a few more dreams. In many ways, Joe came off best. At least he looks fat and happy nowadays whereas there is an infinite sadness in the sight of Ali gripped by debilitating illness.

But both will last the test of time. They have their own place in the history of boxing and those who were present at Madison Square Garden 20 years ago will tell their children and their grandsons what they saw because there hadn't been too much to compare to it before and certainly nothing since.

By comparison, Mason and Lewis were imposters and their contest little more than a charade. Watching them, I was reminded of one of Ali's most telling observations when he asked: "Have you ever thought why all you respectable people are payin' lots of money to see two black boys whuppin' each other? You ought to be ashamed of yourselves."

Twenty years ago in Madison Square Garden the question was rhetorical. Last week at Wembley it was a tough one to answer truthfully without feeling a schmuck.